144, 155

TAKE
CHARGE
OF
YOUR
LIFE

TAKE CHARGE OF YOUR LIFE

by

J. K. Summerhill

CASTLE BOOKS ★ NEW YORK

To the woman
who makes all my work,
all my play, and all my life
so much more worthwhile

Contents

To be always intending to live a new life, but never to find time to set about it—this is as if a man should put off eating and drinking from one day to another, till he be starved and destroyed.

Sir Walter Scott

TAKE CHARGE OF YOUR LIFE

Foreword

Your life begins when you take charge of your life.

Take charge of your life! Without this great factor working for you, you are going to be kicked around, you are going to be a loser. But when you exert CONTROL over the events of your life, you go the way you want to go. You accomplish what you want to accomplish. You have self-confidence, you have drive, you have boundless ability. The more you TAKE CHARGE of your life, the more you take charge of your happiness, your health, your entire life-enjoyment. The more you TAKE CHARGE of your life, the sooner you boost your money-making power higher than you ever dreamed it could be.

Right now—today—start observing the difference between taking charge of your life and being a pushover. Here is a man named X . . . at the age of fifty he earns an apprentice's pay . . . he's tired, he's bitter . . . his wife loyally makes the most of what he brings home, but they know what they are missing. Get to know this type of man and you'll find he never did anything about TAKING CHARGE of his attitudes, his abilities or any other part of his life. At fifty he still doesn't know that a circumstance that means *defeat* to one man can mean *victory* to another. If he never learns how to TAKE CHARGE of his life, he'll never eat anything more than crumbs at life's table.

And here is a man named Y. Week by week he pockets ten times the amount of X's salary, likes his work, takes plenty of vacations and feels fit as a fiddle. Watch him park a handsome car in front of the handsomest house on the block. Watch him walk in with a handsome present for his wife, and later welcome his friends to a plenteous dinner and a bright social evening. *Y is no smarter than*

X, but Y did something about his "fate" and his "luck" in life. Y has no basic gift or talent that X doesn't have, but Y *took charge* and won instead of losing. This type of man enjoys a big, juicy slice of pie at life's table.

So can you. Your life beigns when you TAKE CHARGE OF YOUR LIFE. When you take charge of life-situations and make them go *your* way. When you take charge of certain techniques that make the odds swing in *your* favor.

The method that helps you TAKE CHARGE OF YOUR LIFE

The method that helps you TAKE CHARGE OF YOUR LIFE is founded on ACTION. You perform certain specific, tested actions that reinforce each other with tremendous, cumulative, TAKE–CHARGE power. These actions will change the way you FEEL (or "emote") and the way you THINK.

Through certain actions you can change the way you feel from *discouraged* to *encouraged, cheerful, self-confident.* You can change the way you think from *negative* to *absolutely positive.*

Through certain actions you can change the way you see yourself from *washed up* to *bursting with promise.*

Through certain actions you can change the way you see a life-situation from *This is going to defeat me* into *This is a victory.*

Through certain actions you can change your relations with your fellow men from *full of conflict* into *full of friendship and cooperation.*

And hear this: The way you act, the way you think and the way you feel are so inseparably connected with each other that each one of them always affects the other two.

Feel better and you'll act better.

Think better and you'll feel better.

Act better and you'll think better.

Act better and you'll feel better.

Feel better and you'll think better.

Think better and you'll act better.

The best key, however, is ACTION. A few people can exert direct control over their thoughts and their emotions. But *everyone* can exert nearly 100 per cent control over his conscious actions.

2

Go into action of the right kind and you stir up the entire cycle of your natural success forces. As Aristotle said: "What we have to learn, we learn by doing."

The kind of action you need is TELEOLOGICAL, or goal-seeking, action.

Teleology as a philosophy is concerned with the end of various means, or with *goal*. Thus, man has been described as a teleological or *goal-seeking* animal.

The actions set out in this book are actions directed toward specific goals. They are, therefore, teleological actions. They are simple actions nevertheless—but I want you to remember the word *teleological*. *Goal* is a great word, and I want you to connect it with the more unusual word *teleological*.

The actions set out in this book are actions directed toward specific goals; but your over-all goal is always to TAKE CHARGE OF YOUR LIFE. As you proceed, however, you take actions directed toward interim goals—toward taking charge of certain aspects of your life. These interim goals overlap each other, and each Teleological Action spreads its influence through your *entire* personality, touching *all* your desires, drives and aspirations.

As soon as you finish the first Teleological Action, you are going to feel yourself building, moving, taking hold, TAKING CHARGE, progressing. *At any point in this book, with any one of the forty-three Teleological Actions, you may find your own great breakthrough of success.*

I have seen these seeming miracles. I have helped them happen.

A salesman who was sixty-one years old—still broke after forty years of selling—came to me for advice. We discussed the Teleological Actions he should use and he practiced each Action a few times. Then he couldn't hold himself back; he had to go out and see if the mighty difference he felt in himself was the right kind of difference. It was! That year he doubled his previous income. The next year he doubled that. Now he is earning from six to seven times as much as he did a little while ago. Just as important is the new zest and buoyancy that floods his entire being. He tells me that he used to feel as though he were seventy-five, but now he feels as though he were forty.

I had a few talks with a shop foreman who was having trouble keeping his job. His basic difficulty lay in his relations with his men. I set him up with Teleological Actions, and in just twelve days he had gotten rid of enmity and rivalry in his department. In six weeks he had that department breaking production records. Now he is vice-president in charge of production, and he is "carrying the torch" for my methods—running TAKE CHARGE classes on company time, free to all employees, with guaranteed personal and company profit.

Another man had tried four times to make a retail store pay, and had failed every time. I got to chatting with him when I was buying records for my hi-fi, and found out he didn't want to be someone else's clerk; he wanted to run a record store of his own.

"But I guess I know when I'm licked," he said.

"Hmmmmm," said I. "How about dropping in on me this evening?"

Three days later that man was looking for a new store. Today, four years later, he has two record stores doing a booming business and is getting ready to open a third. Let me make clear that I gave him no money nor did I arrange for him to obtain credit. Teleological Action helped him get financing where it had been refused before. Other Teleological Actions made him a successful merchant where he never could quite "catch on" before.

This man also feels healthier, happier, more friendly with his fellows, more loving with his wife and his family. There is more to life than money; but the man who succeeds in his career builds all the rest of his life to a far better level than the man who does not.

Forty-three life-transforming Teleological Actions are in your hands.

These Actions take charge of your thinking. They take charge of your emotions. They take charge of your very *spirit*. They focus all of you in the way you want to go.

Let me make clear, however, that Teleological Action works its wonders only when you *want* a life filled with achievement and joy.

4

And when you are willing to *do something* toward setting up your own feast at life's great table.

Is this well understood? Are you ready to ACT in your own behalf and in behalf of your loved ones? Let this be so, and you are ready to begin.

Turn to the next page and find out how to take charge of your WILL TO WIN. This is basic in taking charge of your life. For many a man, taking charge of his WILL TO WIN is all he needs. Perhaps this one simple Teleological Action will do the trick for you; one easy, astonishing "TA" that will lift you right out of your chair, full of excitement and determination.

1 Take Firm Control of Your Will to Win

You have a WILL TO WIN and a WILL TO LOSE. Much of your success and your happiness depends upon whether you allow your WILL TO LOSE to hamstring you, or whether you take charge of your WILL TO WIN and drive ahead to victory after victory. A simple action helps you take charge of your WILL TO WIN—an action so easy that you'll be amazed and delighted when you feel it work its wonders.

Harold L. sat down wearily and told me the picture he saw of himself.

"I'm a failure," he concluded.

Because I knew something about him, I knew he had what it takes to make the fifty thousand a year that gives you a very pleasant life, or the hundred thousand that puts you on Easy Street. Right then, however, he could not earn enough take-home pay to support his small family in very modest quarters.

He sat with his head hanging, as though he had a heavy, invisible chain around his neck. In fact he did have something like this, and so does many another man who loses his WILL TO WIN and allows his WILL TO LOSE to be his master.

Harold was in his forties, and he worked in a low, low echelon of a big insurance company. He had tried for a better job, but his superiors were too doubtful about him to allow him to have more responsibility.

Since I handled certain personnel problems for that company, they had sent Harold to see me. "This man has something on the ball but he acts like his own worst enemy," the personnel director had told me. "Maybe you can see what ails him."

Harold's first words—"I'm a failure"—gave me an important clue. "Well now," I said, "you may have failed a few times, but let's look at the other side of the picture."

He laughed bitterly. "What other side? I'm a failure. I'm a flop. That's the story of my life—one failure after another." He told me about his failure in four or five different lines of business. "You don't call that a picture of success, do you?"

"No, looking at the picture the way you paint it, I'd call it a picture of failure. And that's what is holding you back—your portrait of yourself as a failure, a loser. But there is another side to your portrait, if you'll just turn it over. Look at that other side and you'll see a *winner*." He laughed again, the same bitter way, but I persisted. "You'll not only see yourself as the winner you have been, but also you'll recapture the *feeling* of winning. You can go ahead and win again."

"You've got the wrong man."

"Suppose I showed you a simple way to prove to yourself that you have been a winner? Suppose I showed you the record in your own writing, in black and white?" He became interested, and I went on: "Would you be willing to take some action in order to do this? I call it a certain kind of teleological action, that is, action directed toward a goal. The goal is to restore your picture of yourself as a winner, and through that picture restore your WILL TO WIN. Will you take a simple action?"

I explained the action I wanted him to take, which was the same Teleological Action I am going to show you in a moment. He found a number of reasons why it wouldn't work. I was not surprised, since the man who is dominated by his WILL TO LOSE tends to hold onto it. You tend to cling to any habit, however damaging it may be, until you take ACTION to remove it.

Eventually he said he would try my Teleological Action. He did try it the next day, got rather fussed-up, phoned me for a restoration of confidence, then settled down and did it right.

When Harold L. came into my office again, he strode like a conquering hero, no invisible chains bowed him down and he almost shook my hand off. Already he was in a job level above the one previously denied to him! But that was nothing. He had his eye on a much better job, and I could tell by the ring of self-confidence in his voice that he was going to get it. He said that my Teleological Action had taken him by the scruff of his neck and had flung him out of his rut. He wondered now why any man ever acted, felt or thought like a loser when he could act, feel and think like a winner, and reap all the rewards. He said that when you find your WILL TO WIN it's like finding a signpost that puts you on the straight road . . . it's like seeing the lighthouse that brings you into your chosen harbor . . . it's like the map that shows you where your treasure is hidden—right within reach!

Now it's *your* turn to take the same, simple Teleological Action.

Maybe it will be your turn to doubt, at first, that an action so simple can have such far-reaching results. But just try it. The Action is in three parts, and should not take you more than a couple of hours altogether.

Go ahead right now with this first, tremendously important "TA." You have nothing to lose and a new world to win.

TA: PART ONE: MAKE A LIST.

Make a list of a dozen or so incidents in your life wherein you were a *winner*. Anytime, anywhere you were successful—in any way, on any level.

Big success or small success; it makes no difference. Any WIN will do. Here is a list one man drew up. The only thing remarkable about this list is that it is so unremarkable! Yet this same list, as part of the double-barreled TA, got the chains off that man's neck and got him going in a great new career.

> I thought one of the girls in our office would make a wonderful wife for my son. I introduced them, they went for each other, and now they are married and very happy.
>
> My unit at the plant won the yearly Efficiency Award.
>
> We needed the streets repaired in my neighborhood. I took a petition around, and that's the way we got action out of City Hall.

8

My wife said we couldn't afford a trip to see our relatives in Toronto. I set up a "Toronto account" and put something away every week. We took the trip last summer and had the time of our lives.

I hadn't heard from my old friend George in fifteen years. Then he was coming through our town and he looked me up.

Everyone told me little Susie was terrified of strangers, but the first time she saw me, she came and sat in my lap.

I noticed that one of our salesmen's cars had a very cheap radio, not the regular radio manufactured for that car. I checked and found the entire fleet of six had been delivered with those "Micky Mouse" radios. The company had all the radios replaced at the dealer's expense.

I was once a seaman, so I went down to the Boy Scouts to show them how to tie knots. The boys all said they understood my way better than the scoutmaster's.

Nothing tremendous, and Harold L.'s list was no more remarkable. But along with the rest of this TA it certainly did the job for him! The important factor here is *your own black and white RECORD OF WINNING.* You must see that picture of yourself as a person who *has what it takes* to be a WINNER.

Make your list! Search back through your activities at your job, with your family, with your friends, at your hobbies. What have you learned? (Learning something well is a victory.) Have you ever accomplished a task after someone else said you couldn't do it? That is also a very important kind of WINNING.

Make your own list of victories and read it. Do this carefully.

You can recapture and hold that WINNING FEELING.

As you read through your list, pause and relive each event you have listed. You will find this a very pleasant experience. It makes you feel good about yourself. It is an action that gives you, once again, the WINNING FEELING you had at the time of your success. Since your mind can hold only one thought or emotion at a time, you cannot possibly dwell upon failure. You see and you enjoy the picture of yourself as a SUCCESS.

You must try this in order to appreciate it. You must feel the great head-to-toe tonic of that WINNING FEELING as you *relive* the times you WON. It is *very* easy to do this, but don't try to do it all in your mind. Make that written list, because you focus your mind through the action of writing. Read back through the list and flood yourself with your remembered, re-created WINNING FEELING. The more you do this, the more you tend to TAKE CHARGE of that WINNING FEELING and make it a permanent part of your life.

J. C. Penney, who built a huge chain of department stores after some initial failures, spoke of something very like the WINNING FEELING that eventually carried him where he wanted to go.

Henry J. Kaiser has mentioned the same kind of feeling—that which takes hold of a man and sets up success-forces which are well-nigh irresistible.

Even physical skills respond to that WINNING FEELING. A few years ago, when Don Larsen pitched a perfect game in a World Series, he said he had had a "feeling" he would do it.

Every past WIN gives you a WINNING FEELING you can recapture and *carry along* to stand behind future success. And hear this: Your WINNING FEELING is an emotion, and the part of your mind that holds emotion is not the critical part of your mind. The part of your mind that holds emotion does not examine where the emotion came from. *Fear* is *fear,* for example, whether it be fear of a mouse or fear of a tiger. *Anticipation* is *anticipation,* whether you anticipate the arrival of your vacation time or the arrival of a welcome visitor. And *victory* is *victory,* whether it came from winning the spelling medal in the eighth grade, buying a good used car for fifty dollars when everyone said you couldn't, or putting over a million-dollar deal in aluminum window frames. That is why *every* and *any* past WIN can give you that WINNING FEELING to relive, enjoy . . . and *hold onto*.

The gift of holding onto your WINNING FEELING, of finding it always within your mind as a built-in boost toward wealth and happiness, may not come all at once. But your very first try will

10

show you where you are going. As you perform the remainder of the first Teleological Action, and as you go into other Teleological Actions, you will continually strengthen your grip on your WINNING FEELING.

Take action right now to reinforce and take charge of your WINNING FEELING. Go back now to your WIN list.

TA: PART TWO: ADD SPECIFIC WIN-FACTORS TO YOUR LIST.

Take up your pen or pencil and go through your list once more. This time, ask yourself what *winning quality* is inherent in each item. Add a short note to each item, pinning down this winning quality—a quality which, of course, *always stays with you*.

Here is how the sample list looked when the person who made the list added his WIN-FACTORS to it.

> I thought one of the girls in our office would make a wonderful wife for my son. I introduced them, they went for each other, and now they are married and very happy. (I am a good judge of human nature.)

> My unit at the plant won the yearly Efficiency Award. (I am a good man to have on a team.)

> We needed the streets repaired in my neighborhood. I took a petition around, and that's the way we got action out of City Hall. (I don't just sit and complain; I *do something*.)

> My wife said we couldn't afford a trip to see our relatives in Toronto. I set up a "Toronto account" and put something away every week. We took the trip last summer and had the time of our lives. (I have a sense of GOAL and constancy of purpose.)

> I hadn't heard from my old friend George in fifteen years. Then he was coming through our town and he looked me up. (I'm the kind of person who is remembered.)

> Everyone told me little Susie was terrified of strangers,

11

but the first time she saw me, she came and sat in my lap. (I inspire confidence.)

I noticed that one of our salesmen's cars had a very cheap radio, not the regular radio manufactured for that car. I checked and found the entire fleet of six had been delivered with those "Mickey Mouse" radios. The company had all the radios replaced at the dealer's expense. (I can smell out a fraud.)

I was once a seaman, so I went down to the Boy Scouts to show them how to tie knots. The boys all said they understood my way better than the scoutmaster's. (I'm a good teacher.)

Well, if you were the person who had made the list, you'd see you have quite a bit going for you:

I am a good judge of human nature.
I am a good man to have on a team.
I don't just sit and complain; I do something.
I have a sense of GOAL and constancy of purpose.
I'm the kind of person who is remembered.
I inspire confidence.
I can smell out a fraud.
I'm a good teacher.

Add specific WIN–FACTORS to your own list and you may whistle in amazement at the picture of yourself. For you have a great deal with which to build your success, and you have scarcely begun to see it! EVERYONE is filled with the qualities that WIN; but those qualities do nothing for you when they lie dormant. You must wake them up, believe in them, exercise them, *want* those priceless human qualities to go to work for you. That's when you really pave the road that leads to your dearest dreams.

Your mood of success is backed up with the solid building blocks that success is made of.

Now let us move into Part Three of the Teleological Action that so mightily strengthens your WILL TO WIN.

Write a friendly, informal letter as though you were writing to a stranger who knew nothing about you, and you wanted to tell him something about yourself. The stranger needs no name; let's call him Mr. X.

Your letter will be friendly, informal and rather chatty; and above all it will be a *point-of-view* letter, heavily slanted toward revealing your record of success.

Never mind modesty! Your purpose in writing to Mr. X is to tell him about a dozen or so occasions in your life when you definitely WON, and WON because you possessed important winning qualities which you will make very clear to him. The entire tone of your letter will be that of a person who enjoys an all-around pattern of life-success.

You have made your list, you added WIN–FACTORS to it, so you are ready to write your letter. Sit down and do it. First write a draft on scrap paper, and read it over before you write a final draft. You may write your point-of-view letter in any way you wish, but here is a model that has proved helpful to many:

> Dear Mr. X:
> It's a pleasure to make a pen pal, and I want to tell you something about myself. I am glad to say I have had a good deal of success in my life. To mention just a few incidents . . .

Here you fill in the items from the WIN-list you made. But tell them informally; for example:

> My unit won the Efficiency Award, and it felt very good to know I'm the right kind of man to have on a team. And then there was the time my friend George came through town and looked me up after fifteen years of being out of communication. Imagine, fifteen years without hearing a word from each other, yet he felt he just had to say Hello to me. It's great to know you are a person who is remembered. . . .

13

And so forth. As you go along, you will almost certainly recall other times when your qualities of success came through, and you may add them to your list; or if you have too many, jot them down in case you want to write another letter. Tell no lies. Invent nothing. Give Mr. X an impression of *a life filled with joyful achievement*. And end on a high note, like this:

> It certainly feels fine to look back upon one's record of success. It reminds you that you are still the same person who performed so well on so many occasions, so you can go right ahead and succeed today and succeed again tomorrow.
>
> Sincerely,
(your name)

After you write your first draft, go over it carefully. Make sure the entire letter gives a single impression: *The writer is happily involved in a life filled with WINNING*. Put a lift in every line.

Then write your final draft. Use pen or typewriter, write on your best stationery and make it neat. Remember, you are writing to a person to whom you wish to display SUCCESS. Let the very appearance of your letter proclaim that it comes from a consistently successful person. As you begin to write your final draft, however: *Make an important change in the salutation.*

Do not write to Mr. X. Instead, write to *yourself*. Do it exactly that way: first write a draft of your letter to Mr. X, a stranger; then write the final draft to *yourself*.

When the letter is sincere and well written, fold it into an envelope, address the envelope to yourself, seal it, stamp it. Take it down to the corner and drop it into the mailbox. Hear the satisfying *clang* as the mailbox lid closes on the most important letter of your life.

**The miracle that happens when you open your
point-of-view letter**

Your letter will come back to you in a day or two, but do not open it the day it arrives. Let another two or three days go by. The

14

letter will go "out of your mind." Then, three or four days after you wrote it, you'll become anxious to read it.

Be sure you are alone when you read the point-of-view letter you sent to that stranger who is yourself.

Read it slowly, word by word.

Gradually, as you read, a sense of glad wonderment and astonished delight begins to sing within your being. "Now . . . wait . . . a . . . minute!" says many a person as he reads his own letter. "Is this me?"

Then with a great surge of delight you realize it *is* you, a gloriously gleaming facet of YOU, at last unclouded and *recognized*. Be sure you are alone when you read your own letter because the power of self-revelation is terrific. Men have told me they spent an hour striding up and down, reading the letter over and over. Some said frankly they found tears in their eyes. But there it is on the record and it is YOU. It is your third meeting with your WILL TO WIN and it hits the hardest. *Of course* you always have had the power to make situations come out YOUR way. *Of course* you have every success-quality that belongs to any other man. *Of course* you can push the WILL TO LOSE down, away, far out of your life, hold the WILL TO WIN and build upon it magnificently.

They acted and achieved with their WILL TO WIN.

I mentioned earlier that any Teleological Action, anywhere in this book, might give you *your* great breakthrough.

In some cases that breakthrough comes right here. A man fills himself with that WINNING FEELING, takes charge of his WILL TO WIN like a football player taking charge of a loose football— and runs with it!

A man I know had once been interested in buying up various items of Army surplus and selling them by mail. He had got started in this as a part-time business, but his family discouraged him and he allowed the business to fade away. Many years later, when I was "field-testing" the various components of this book, he took the Teleological Action explained in this chapter: he made a list of WIN-items, added WIN–FACTORS to it, incorporated the list in a point-of-view letter, read the letter.

15

Suddenly he relived the WINNING FEELING. Why had he ever given up his business? Why had he allowed other people to force their own defeatism—their WILL TO LOSE—upon him? Inspired and aglow, he wrote immediately for catalogues of surplus material. In three months he was getting orders and in six months he was making more than the amount of his salary on his regular job. Soon he was able to quit his job. Now he is the prosperous head of a mail-order business that is a roaring success.

An entirely different type of person, a high-school principal, also tested the same Teleological Action that wakes up your WILL TO WIN. This man's great ambition was to become state superintendent of education. He had become stuck in a backward school district, however, in a grim little town where there was little respect for education. The school and its books and equipment were in miserable shape, and so was the school's scholastic record.

"I put most of my energy into being sorry for myself," the principal told me later. "But then my point-of-view letter came back to me and I read it . . ."

He leaped from his chair, shouting: "What's the matter with me?" He went to the telephone and called the head of the school board. He insisted the board call a special meeting, at which he raised hell until he got money enough for sufficient textbooks and a decent library in his school. When he could not get an appropriation for needed furniture, he organized a furniture bee. Volunteers built benches and desks in the school shop, knocking off now and then for coffee and cake and dancing in the gymnasium. Going ahead with other projects in the same all-alive new spirit, he made a vital go-go place out of that high school. He raised average marks by 12 per cent, college entrances by 14 per cent. Soon he was district superintendent and I know he will one day be state superintendent of education with vast benefit to all concerned.

"How can I recognize the WILL TO LOSE?"

I quote the question because so many people ask it. At one time I refused to admit there is such a thing as the WILL TO LOSE; but it's there, all right. It is akin to the death-wish that lurks in the human psyche, just as the WILL TO WIN is akin to the life-wish we also possess.

There was a time in prehistory when man needed a very strong life-wish just to stay alive. In civilization, however, we make allowances for our weaker people, so you can still cherish your WILL TO LOSE while you manage to stay alive and earn some kind of living.

As for *recognizing* those who see only the failure side of themselves, and do their best to live the picture they see, you will find there is a general pattern. Bear in mind that most losers get a strange, backward-oriented *satisfaction* out of losing. After all, when you live at a low level, you can hardly fall very far. True, you do not have the stimulation and reward that come with winning. But then, you *take no risks*.

The dedicated loser may get some blame from his wife for not putting enough meat on the table. But contrast this with the plight of a company president who goofs away a million dollars!

A loser may see his friends rise to better jobs, higher pay and richer living. But wait till one of those high-rising friends can't get the work out of his staff and he is held responsible! Then it's so *good* to have your feet firmly welded to the bottom of the ladder.

Sometimes a loser may rise a couple of rungs. Yet you can almost see his cutoff point—the point beyond which he would rather not go. Because it often represents a point at which he once got hurt, he won't risk getting hurt again. His WILL TO LOSE now informs him: "You've stuck your neck out far enough!"

To recognize the willing loser, watch for two highly significant personal characteristics. They do not seem at all the same, but their roots are the same, and at different times you may see them in the same person.

1. Watch for the cheerful, rather lovable loser. Generally he'll have decades of ill-paid work behind him and so he feels entitled to say: "Well, I tried!" (He never really tried, but that's beside the point.) He has plenty of company among those who "tried," and they never berate each other for the half-baked "try" that has LOSE built into it. This man may be a very helpful person, perhaps a homespun philosopher who has trained himself to laugh at money; and he will usually be so lovable and kindly that you simply have

17

to forgive him his shortcomings. And that is what he wants. Underneath, he doesn't like himself, and he has to show the world that at least he is good at being lovable.

2. Watch for that self-dislike when it becomes self-hate. The self-hater turns his hatred upon those who are successful, sneers at them, snarls at them, *damages them when he can*.

This was brought home to a man who had just become a foreman in a radio factory and now exerted authority over a group of men who had been his work-equals for many years. The foreman would check his inventory through the reports that came from the stockroom, then tell the plant manager he had enough parts to fill an order; then, with the production line going, he'd suddenly find a shortage of transistors or whatnot. I almost had to hit him on the head before he would believe that one of his old friends was sabotaging him with false inventory records. The old friend was jealous of the foreman's success; he had also been hearing from his own wife about their need for more money—and a frustrated person tends to strike back.

Typically, too, the loser will claim all kinds of virtues for just "making a living" and no more. He will tell you to stay out of the higher-up rat race and you'll live longer. Forbear to remind him that United States Public Health Service records show that men in the upper income brackets are the ones who live longer.

Likewise will the devotee of the WILL TO LOSE tell you that becoming successful is bad for the character; it turns a man into an s.o.b. It does happen now and then, but the statement is the merest wishful thinking. Success, because it takes away frustration, worry and the feeling of inferiority, most often gives the successful man a tolerance of others. Looking back over more than forty years of being in business, I know I have never found more than one s.o.b. among any ten successful men. Among those who failed, however, I'd find, in any ten, at least five who barked at their mothers.

One more point about devoted losers: They generally have mixed-up ideas about the relationship between work and play.

I am thinking of a young man I once hired to help me sell ranch homes near a golf course in Florida. His job was to be out there taking care of people who wanted to see the homes while I took

18

care of the office. When I found out he spent a good many working hours playing golf, I told him that of course he was fired; but also, I said, I was concerned about him. Where did he think he'd go in his career if he didn't know the difference between work and play? I even quoted from the Talmud: "Great is work which lends dignity to man."

At that point I was bitterly denounced. It seemed I was too old-fashioned to know how important it is for a man to relax from his work. But as I watched the furious young man drive out of my life, I recalled that I had seen this same phenomenon in others who prefer to lose: you can cut down their workday to four hours (I have nothing against short workdays) and still their interest is not in the constructive effort that makes some contribution to society and to themselves; their interest is in being *relieved* of constructive effort. They can never take the pleasure in relaxation that comes when rest is well earned; they can rarely afford to finance their leisure with good equipment or travel, so they lose all around. But then, they are losers; and when you set up a portrait of yourself as a loser, you simply can't help living up to it.

Well? How do *you* rate on that list of *symptoms of the WILL TO LOSE?*

If you now realize you are cherishing your WILL TO LOSE, and neglecting your WILL TO WIN, don't go off into agonized soul-searching.

It is not necessary and will probably do you no good. Instead, go into ACTION. Even if you cannot find the WILL TO LOSE in yourself, but still find you cannot make your life what you want it to be, go into ACTION—Teleological Action that makes the WILL TO WIN rise from the depths of your being, step front-center and say "Let's go!"

Take charge of your WILL TO WIN and it will fill your mind so that you are constantly impelled toward every further business action or personal action that brings VICTORY. You will never stop yourself with the feeble gesture; you will never sound off with the feeble excuse. You know you are a WINNER. Every dynamic of your mind and body will work energetically to fulfill the picture you see of yourself—the picture of a WINNER.

Go ahead! Make your list. Write your letter.

Some will delay and doubt and hesitate till they lose sight of the entire concept of the WILL TO WIN. They are the ones who find their WILL TO LOSE too comfortable to be abandoned.

Others will realize that a new, high-level life—a top-flight career and a really dramatic increase in their earning and spending power —cannot be achieved by merely hoping. You have to *do* something to lift your life out of the shadows and into the sunshine.

I strongly suggest that you make your list and write your letter before you go on to Chapter II. Psychologically, you are in a much stronger position when you make progress *quickly*—as you will.

By this time you will undoubtedly recall dozens of WIN experiences. The best procedure is: *Write more letters.* Write as many letters as you wish. But follow the same steps each time: first the list, then the addition of WIN–FACTORS, then the letter with the first draft to Mister X and the second draft to YOU.

Keep your WIN–FACTORS all together on a separate list, for instant reference. Here are a few more WIN–FACTORS that people found in themselves—to their utter astonishment and delight.

I can organize scattered bits of information.

I can show people what's wrong with their work and still remain friends with them.

I can overcome small irritations and not let them get me down.

I can pretty well predict what other people will do under given circumstances.

I am not afraid of new ideas.

Most of the advice I give turns out to be right.

When I don't know how to do something, I am willing to take the trouble to find out.

20

All based on the most ordinary events . . . and all serving to back up and strengthen the FEELING OF WINNING.

Make your list.
Write your letter.
Do it NOW.

Where we have been:

Many a failure is not the victim of circumstances, not the victim of anything but his own WILL TO LOSE. He submerges his WILL TO WIN. He paints a portrait of himself as a loser, and that is the portrait he lives up to.

The WILL TO WIN is brought forward and you take charge of it by Teleological Action. First you make a list of WIN-items. These may be small victories but they give you a new picture of yourself as a winner. Back up this picture with WIN—FACTORS that show you that you really have what it takes to be a winner.

Then write yourself a letter that once again confirms your new self-portrait. Find the FEELING OF WINNING, hold onto it, know it will increase tremendously as you go along—and will always stand by you to help you win and win and win again.

What are the symptoms of the WILL TO LOSE? You see how to recognize them in yourself and others. You may realize how much you have lost to the WILL TO LOSE. But you do not blame or berate yourself. Go into ACTION, take charge of your WILL TO WIN, start building the foundations of your great new life right here, right now.

Where we are going:

The next chapter deals with a peculiarly downgrading habit that afflicts some people. Once again, through easy Teleological Action, you'll see how to change a bad habit into a good habit, how to add power and progress as you increasingly TAKE CHARGE OF YOUR LIFE.

2 Get a Grip on Your Self-Respect

You take Teleological Action toward making yourself always feel worthy of the best in life. You get rid of a bad habit that keeps men from their goals. You win instant results in getting better service, more respect from others, and more advancement. This leads you to apply the magic of self-respect and WIN at higher and higher levels.

Try the following experiment, and you'll find out something about human nature.

Pick out three or four people with whom you are fairly well acquainted. Choose people who are not overly fond of the Will to Win. You won't have any trouble in finding such people.

Tell each of these people about some exciting ambition that seethes in your mind. Tell each of them separately and enthusiastically about some goal you have set up. Let's say you have decided to become the manager of an enormous department store. Your title right now may be Second Assistant Buyer-in-Training, but you say to your friends: "One day I am going to be manager."

You will be broadly grinned at, and told to stop kidding. You may get a patronizing pat on the back and be told to go on dreaming.

Now say the same thing to the manager: "Mr. Manager, one day *I* am going to be manager of this store." Say this sincerely and enthusiastically, just as you said it to your friends. And watch the difference in the manager's reaction. Whatever he may reply, he will not laugh at you. And he will never say anything like "Go on dreaming."

Men who have achieved do not laugh at those who dream of

achievement. The man at the top knows he had to see his goal in his own mind before he turned it into reality. The dream, the plan, the concept of the goal, comes first, and when the man at the top hears that a man in a lower position has a man-sized goal, those two men have something in common.

Your goals and the way you conceive of them are of the greatest importance in building a better life. In this chapter I'll show you how to build a basic strength that makes you *capable* of conceiving great goals and *capable* of driving toward them.

This is the great basic strength called SELF-RESPECT. My dictionary says that self-respect is "laudable self-esteem." Let's hold onto that word *laudable* and remember that self-respect is not inflated self-importance. Self-respect, we may say, is your innate conviction that it is *right* for you to receive large, juicy slices of pie at life's table.

Self-respect is priceless in small matters.

Like its close relation the Will to Win, self-respect is as priceless in small matters as in million-dollar ones. Like the Will to Win, self-respect builds itself more and more strongly the more you exercise it—anywhere, anytime, at any level.

So I invite you to look at the roots of your self-respect in several average patterns of circumstance. You can then extend these average patterns into the specific circumstances of your own life, however important or critical these areas may be. A man who is self-respecting in the bosom of his family is self-respecting among his business associates. A man who asks for a match in a self-respecting manner will ask for a ten-thousand-dollar raise in a self-respecting manner.

Your Teleological Action toward taking charge of your self-respect is oriented differently from that of your Will to Win. The basic principle, however, is the same: ACT with self-respect and you will soon THINK like a self-respecting person and FEEL like a self-respecting person. Your thoughts and feelings then make it all the more natural and inevitable that you will act with self-respect in every life-situation, as though you feel worthy of receiving the best life has to offer. And *expecting* the best in life is a mighty aid in getting it!

23

Stop saying KICK ME.

That is the major reason why so many people get kicked around by life instead of being able to gather in all that is pleasant and rewarding. In their inmost spirits they say: KICK ME!

When I was a boy in the lower grades, my friends and I used to inflict various embarrassments upon one another. We rejoiced in the thumbtack on the seat, the wet blackboard sponge in the coat sleeve, the tin can tied to the bicycle, the pages of a school book pasted together. And we rejoiced most greatly in the sign, crudely lettered on cardboard, that proclaimed: KICK ME. When another boy's back was turned, you could pin such a sign to the slack of his corduroy knickerbockers without his knowing it. Then, with great glee, you kicked him. When he protested, you showed him the sign. He'd gotten what he asked for, hadn't he?

The bruises fade, the KICK ME signs are put away with other childish things, and I am sure there is no literal carry-over in the adult personality, which is formed in more subtle ways. But millions upon millions of adults still say KICK ME in one way or another—and get what they ask for. For the sake of your self-respect, start right now to kick the habit of saying KICK ME!

TA: PART ONE: SHOW SELF-RESPECT IN A SERVICE SITUATION.

Here is a man buying a pipe. There are many varieties of pipes, and understandably he will suit his own taste in shape, size, color and so forth. But when this man asks the clerk to let him see a meerschaum instead of a brier, he cringes and adds: "I hate to be a nuisance." And when he wants to see a different brand he winces and says: "I'm sorry to take your time."

This man is saying KICK ME. I have spoken to hundreds of retail salesmen and saleswomen, and they invariably agree that they are annoyed by shoppers who don't have self-respect. Also, if the sales people are lazy or tired or rushed—or simply sufficiently annoyed—they will not give such a shopper the service they would give to a shopper who respects himself. The person who *expects* to be well served *is* well served. He is also more likely to buy what he

24

wants and he can often make his money go further. The KICK ME type expects the worst and gets it.

Naturally you do not ask an outrageous amount of service from anyone who serves you. This kind of thing goes along with the fussy self-importance that often betrays the inferiority hiding underneath. Lack of respect for a sales person or anyone else from whom you ask service is, in a way, a lack of self-respect.

As one perceptive saleswoman put it: "Don't we all serve each other in some way? There is nothing second-class about serving or about being served."

I have also interviewed many secretaries to see what kind of bosses get their best work out of them. They don't like the *demander*. And they don't like the boss who seems afraid to ask for service. "Why," asked one girl, "should my boss say: 'Get me the Jones file if you don't mind'? That's my job, isn't it?"

The kind of boss voted *best* would say: "Get me the Jones file, please," or even leave out the please, but always speak courteously and with no implied apology in his tone. That kind of boss is well served and his secretary likes him.

Along the lines of service situations, I am reminded of a rather extraordinary one. I once paused to say Good Morning to our lifeguard on a California beach. He smiled, but his smile faded as he glanced beyond me. Obviously he was bothered by the sight of a man who was approaching.

"There's that fellow coming to thank me again!" the lifeguard groaned. "He got into trouble in the surf a couple of weeks ago, and I pulled him out. Now he thanks me a dozen times a day for saving his life. He's a pain. He acts as though his life weren't worth saving."

He acts as though his life weren't worth saving! Think about that.

What to do when you don't get the service you're entitled to.

You are a self-respecting person and you don't get the service you should get. You'd like to get that service without making a scene about it. Do this: Act toward the serving person as though you know he has a customarily high standard of service, but you understand that anyone can slip.

25

This is a very powerful lever in human relations. You are showing the other person a picture of himself that you expect him to live up to—and he is impelled to live up to it.

Thus, to the lazy filling-station attendant, you say with a smile: "You *were* going to wipe my windshield, weren't you?" It gets wiped.

To the waiter who would rather chat with the cashier than fill your water glass, you say: "Everything's fine on this table . . . except . . . the water?" And you slake your thirst.

Merely be sure you are asking the proper service of the proper person, and your courteous self-respect will get you well served by storekeepers, gasoline pumpers, waiters, bank tellers, bartenders and everybody else, including policemen.

Get the KICK ME out of your voice! Get the KICK ME out of your words! Get the KICK ME out of your manner! Remember, *the self-respect you build stays with you.* The self-respect that shows in your personality may get you the right kind of shoelace today and the right kind of great lifetime career tomorrow.

TA: PART TWO: SHOW SELF-RESPECT IN THE WORK YOU DO.

Andy wanted a career in advertising, and got a job as copy cub in an advertising agency. But Andy was a KICK ME type. His lack of self-respect always had him in trouble with the copy chief. It was not that his work was really bad, although it showed his lack of experience. It was his attitude toward the copy he wrote. As he handed the copy chief a piece of copy, he would also pass along a self-deprecating giggle, a feeble heh-heh-heh which meant: *Of course I know how silly it is to pretend I can write an ad.* The copy chief gritted his teeth every time.

One day the copy chief blew up and fired Andy. I sat down with the woebegone ex-cub. I got him to see that a *beginner* who does his best is, first and foremost, a *person* who does his best. His work is therefore to be respected even if it has to be corrected. Expertise comes in time. It is in the recognition of *essential worthiness* that both the man and his work get their chance to grow.

I have seen this unfortunate KICK ME attitude stay with a man all his working days. What it comes down to is that he never becomes expert in anything because he stops attempting to lift his work above the KICK ME stage. There is always something tentative and unfinished about any job he does. You can see the connection with the Will to Lose. Such a man never hands in a piece of work with the feeling that *I've done a complete and honest job and I'll stand by it*. To do this would put him out on a limb. So, in order to live up to his picture of himself as a loser, he hands in a job that he *knows* needs correction, and says as much. And he is neither well liked nor well respected nor well rewarded.

On the other hand, when you show your respect toward your own work, you make sure it is worthy of other people's respect as well. You see yourself as a person who does respect-worthy jobs and automatically, without conscious thought, you do all you can to live up to *that* image.

The difference in your progress, your earnings and your success can be like the difference between night and day. And the self-respect you see in an office boy is no different from the self-respect you see in the chairman of the board—and is just as important.

The way you act is the way you feel is the way you think is the way you act is the way you feel is the way you think is the way you act. Keep the KICK ME out of that all-important cycle.

TA: PART THREE: PRACTICE SAYING "I LIKE IT THAT WAY."

In counseling people on ways to bring purpose and progress into their lives, I run into some wacked-up characters. All I can do for them is to send them to a psychiatrist for professional treatment. Such people I think of as "patients." And it's quite remarkable how many of these "patients" have carried the KICK ME habit right over the border. They are in constant retreat. They haven't faith in their ability to call a dog a dog or a cat a cat.

Here is a "patient" who takes twenty minutes to tell me why she had spent her vacation at the mountains instead of at the seashore. Here is a "patient" who takes more than twenty minutes to explain why he is wearing a tie that does not match his suit; but I must *honest-to-God* believe it matches the rest of his wardrobe. Nobody attacked these people but they had to defend themselves against an imagined attack (a sure sign of inner turmoil). Although I kept

27

quiet, they more and more vehemently defended their (to them) all-important actions, continually showing their own doubt of their worthiness to make a decision and continually wanting to be kicked because they had gone ahead and made one.

When I meet the occasional person who is simply too mixed up to be guided toward self-help, I send him to the head-man. Nevertheless, I have successfully guided many a person who had a pretty good grip on himself but who still was in trouble because he never believed that his mere *preference,* and no more, could be reason enough for many of his actions. Such people can have no confidence in themselves, nor trust their own actions. Again, it is a kind of living in a state of retreat. These men are quite consistently kicked by others who want things done *their* way. They can't set up goals, much less attain goals, and they go through life explaining themselves away, apologizing, in short, for taking charge of their own God-given freedom to *be* themselves.

Your right to say "I like it that way" begins at a very basic level—at what I call the cup-of-coffee level. I shall present just one scene to show the invasion of rights that goes on at this level and leave it to you to extend the general pattern into your own affairs.

"No, thank you."

Fond Mamma, whom you love, asks you to have a cup of coffee. You have upon many an occasion enjoyed her excellent coffee, and you tell her this; but at the moment you do not wish to drink a cup of coffee; you tell her this and express your thanks for the offer.

And lo! Fond Mamma decides you *should* have a cup of coffee, pours it and sets it before you.

Fond Mamma may be anybody. The cup of coffee may be any kind of food, drink, goods or service. You may sometimes decide to accept the object or the service merely to please the other party; you must judge the circumstance for yourself. But any person who *consistently* accepts anything forced upon him is saying KICK ME; and again, you can get well kicked at any level of your affairs. And you will!

Stop the tendency right down there at the cup-of-coffee level. If you are dealing with a real Fond Mamma you need not say: "I will not drink this coffee because I said I don't want coffee and I want it that way." Simply act out your right to take charge of what goes down your own throat. Do not drink the coffee. If you are pressed to drink it, smile and repeat courteously: "No, thank you." And *don't* go off into excuses such as "I'm too full" or anything of the sort. This implies the existence of a temporary inhibiting condition, rather than the existence of your four-square *right* to like it that way.

(Presumably you will not drive through red lights because you like it that way, or write your own medical prescriptions if you are not an M.D. Presumably we are all aware of our social responsibilities. In order to do everything the way you like it, you'd have to live quite alone on this earth.)

Resisting at the trampler level.

Sarah, a spinster, was proud of her own little apartment. But she lived near her married brother, and somehow she often found herself doing the housework over there while her childless sister-in-law attended an interior decorating course.

Her brother borrowed from Sarah's rainy-day fund and never got around to repaying. Sister-in-law insisted on redecorating Sarah's apartment; Sarah didn't like the results but accepted them. All this had started on a cup-of-coffee level, but when the pattern gets going, it tends to grow worse.

Concurrently Sarah was having troubles in her office, partly stemming from a taut perfectionism that she ruefully called her "old maid personality." When I heard her story, it seemed to me she was overcompensating in the office for the trampling she took at home. We talked things over. I pointed out to Sarah what she had done to herself by saying KICK ME. I discussed the effect of KICK ME on one's self-respect, the need to take charge of one's self-respect and the great value of an honest *I like it that way.*

Next scene: Sister-in-law is indignant. Sarah has redecorated her apartment to suit herself! And why? Because she likes it that way!

Next scene: Sarah's lease runs out and she moves to the other end of town because she likes it that way.

This led to a glorious breakthrough of self-respect. It led to a

29

change of office character too, and Sarah is now a far more relaxed and tolerant person. She dresses better, looks better, feels better. She has asked her brother to start paying back what he owes her, and she asked him in so quietly definite a tone that he is mailing her a check every pay day. Having stepped out of her "spinster-forever" role, she has joined a hiking club, and I hear that a pleasant widower often is at her side, helping her wear down the high Sierras.

Say it to yourself: *I like it that way*.

Write the five fateful words on a card, carry the card in your pocket, take out the card and read it a dozen times a day: *I like it that way*.

Those five words stir you up. Suddenly you may realize how many kicks you are getting because you don't say *I like it that way* . . . at the cup-of-coffee level, at the trampler level, at the service level . . . in personal matters, business matters, any matters.

Those five words have been breakthrough words for a good many people. Say them! ACT THEM OUT. Courteously and logically show you know how to be the self-respecting *self* you are so very much entitled to be.

TA: PART FOUR: HOLD BACK ON EXPLANATIONS AND APOLOGIES.

You have already seen that a KICK ME attitude often associates itself with a need to explain oneself away. This habit is so widespread, so *un*self-respecting and so damaging to your success that it gets special billing. *Hold back on explanations and apologies*.

Don't cut them out. Certainly there are times when an explanation of your actions is called for. There are also times—far more rare—when an apology is called for. But take a long look at yourself and see if you are not caught up in the damaging, self-downgrading, antisuccess habit of *explaining yourself away* and/or *apologizing your way through life*. If you have this habit, believe me, it is a broad bulwark of the dreadful KICK ME habit, and as a habit you should wipe it right out of your thoughts, feelings and actions.

STOP before you start explaining why you did something or why you made a certain choice.

You like it that way. DO YOU NEED ANY OTHER REASON?

All right, you decide you do owe some kind of explanation. Make it brief. Give the over-all picture, not every painful detail.

You'll be helped to STOP before explaining yourself away if you notice one thing: Any action you perform or any choice you make may be perfectly acceptable to the other fellow—he'd never dream of questioning your rights—*until you start explaining.* This is the entering wedge. He begins to question your *explanation.*

Tell Fond Mamma you don't want a cup of her excellent coffee, thank you, and you are in a self-respecting position of strength.

Tell her you are "too full" and she can plunge right in and find out what you ate for lunch and take you to task for it. That's not what you bargained for when you chose not to have a cup of coffee.

The situation is analogous to being on the receiving end of a strong selling effort. You are pressed to buy something you do not want. The salesman cannot prevail against your simple, strong, courteous refusal to buy, period. But if you start giving him *reasons,* he jumps on your reasons. He has been trained to turn objections into sales. Notice how a determined salesman will often *suggest* reasons you won't buy, hoping to get you to agree. Then he KICKS the reason with a few well-practiced phrases and you feel foolish if you don't sign on the dotted line.

As for *apologies* and their relation to your self-respect: One of the best Teleological Actions in this area is: STOP any apology for little, understandable fumbles that do no harm. *Don't* apologize, in word or manner, for being awkward now and then. So long as you hurt nobody, you are entitled to meet the world with the understanding that a small margin for error helps us all to get along in life.

Suppose you are looking for a job. You sit down at the interviewer's desk, and as you hand him your résumé you knock a pencil off his desk.

If you want to show that interviewer a lack of self-respect that may cost you the job, start by saying: "Oh, how stupid of me! How could I be so clumsy! I am so *very* sorry." And as you scrabble madly to pick up the rolling pencil: "I must apologize for my clumsiness. I am so terribly sorry." And as you rush to restore it to the desk: "Dreadfully sorry!" Then perch on the edge of your chair as though waiting to repair some other damage you expect to do.

If you wish rather to show the self-respect that goes along with good working habits and a sense of Goal, murmur a small "Oh" or say nothing at all. Retrieve the pencil without resembling a cat chasing a mouse. Put it on the desk quite calmly. Sit back in your chair.

Do you see yourself as a cringer, a whiner . . . or as a person who looks the world in the eye? There is an essential and welcome democracy in self-respect. I know I have always preferred to give a job to, or do business with or buy from someone who conducted himself in every way as though he were my equal. Perhaps not my equal in particular knowledge or particular achievement or particular ability—but my equal *as a human being*.

STOP SAYING *KICK ME*. "Beware of what you want, for you are likely to get it," Emerson said. There may be no KICK ME sign pinned to the seat of your pants, but you'll still get kicked when your *picture of yourself* says KICK ME.

You are as big inside as you act outside.

A foundation stone of self-respect is your own respect for *everything* you do. Call it old-fashioned probity. You are honest, you are fair, you are BIG in what you do. Did you perform some dishonest pettiness today? Perhaps not sufficiently dishonest to justify calling the police—but dishonest to your own self-respect?

You are as big inside as you act outside. Do you waste your company's paper towels because you don't have to pay for them? That is petty. You're bigger than that.

You give a five-dollar bill to a restaurant cashier and you receive change for a ten-dollar bill. Do you keep the extra five dollars? It won't make you rich. It is more likely to make you poor because it downgrades your own self-image; it is small; it is petty.

Do you ever "forget" to tip a waiter or waitress because you know you'll never come through that town again? You owe more than a tip to your self-respect.

If you hire a car and pay a dollar or two extra to get non-deductible collision insurance, do you then deliberately dent and scratch the car because you won't have to pay for the damage?

That's a small kind of acting, mister. How big is your *thinking* and your *goal-seeking* if you do that kind of thing?

Do you habitually chisel cigarettes? 'Nuff said.

Do you try to get free legal or medical advice from your lawyer or doctor in the course of "social" conversation? (A self-respecting person who happens to be broke goes to the Legal Aid Society or to a clinic. And by the way, being broke need not hurt your self-respect because you know it's a temporary condition . . . it's being *poor* that can settle down as a damaging self-image.)

Do you ever try to read the papers on someone else's desk while you are doing business with him? This puts you in a class with Peeping Tom.

Do you tell people you wrote to them or sent them a payment or telephoned them when you didn't—but they can't prove you didn't? Heh-heh-heh, it's a little white lie . . . or is it a very small soul wriggling into a dark corner?

You are as big inside as you act outside. A man's bigness *shows* in the man.

I am reminded of a movie that was made from that great story by Stephen Vincent Benet, *The Devil and Daniel Webster*. The Devil, in human guise, displays a soul he has just collected. It is the soul of the town miser, and we see something like a small moth fluttering in the soul-collecting box. "But if only I had Daniel Webster's soul!" exclaims the Devil as nearly as I remember. "His soul would have the wingspread of an eagle!"

Without going into religion, you know what *soul* means. Or call it anything else you wish; your *psyche* or your *ego*. How big is it?

As big as you make it, my friend.

The bigger you build yourself inside, the bigger you act and the bigger you achieve. The smaller you build yourself inside, the smaller you make your life.

You have kicked out KICK ME. Fine! But you're not finished. Stop KICKING YOURSELF. Every petty, dishonest or semi-dishonest act erodes your self-respect, smears mud on your self-image. There is more to self-respect than "standing up for your rights." Self-respect has an inward-seeking side that is every bit as important.

1. Take charge of your self-respect as you face the world.
2. Take charge of your self-respect as you face yourself.

Man, you have success-powers that can help you almost with the magic of Aladdin's lamp. And it is always YOU who must *bring to an effective focus* your own unlimited abilities.

Where we have been:
Unsuccessful people laugh at those who plan for high success, but big men welcome big thinkers. Your goals and the way you conceive them are of great importance. Your self-respect makes you capable of conceiving greatly and building your concepts into solid attainments.

Stop the self-destroying KICK ME habit. Take charge of your self-respect in service situations by expecting to get good service, and you will. Get good service by setting up a good self-image for the other fellow to fulfill. We all serve each other. Society is built on give-and-take.

Nourish your self-respect by respecting the work you do. You will then make sure it is worthy of others' respect as well. Nourish your self-respect by realizing you have a right to "like it that way" in many of your actions and choices. Start respecting your right of choice at the cup-of-coffee level and you'll use it effectively at any level.

Hold back on explanations and apologies except where they are really needed. Note how explanation runs into apology, how an unneeded explanation puts you in a weak position when silence can keep you strong. In the great democracy of self-respect, small errors won't hurt you if you don't attempt to apologize for them.

You are as big inside as you act outside. Don't erode your self-respect with petty, semidishonest actions. Take charge of your self-respect as you face the world. Take charge of your self-respect as you face yourself. Your self-respect is strongly keyed to your success-power.

Where we are going:
In the next chapter you add the power of *direction* to your ambition. You see the "how" of a TAKE–CHARGE procedure that makes a great deal else fall in line.

34

3 Energize Your Full Goal-Winning Power

When you know where you are going, every step becomes a step in the right direction. When you know what you want to buy with the money you make, it helps you to make more money—and helps you find happiness that is warmly your own. Know your long-term goals and the interim goals that get you there; how to make your goals so real and vivid that you automatically strengthen the abilities that gather them in.

Quite often I meet men who have earned a good deal of money. Only now and then, however, do I meet a man who is really happy in the way he *spends* his money. I keep thinking back on such men. They are fulfilled. They are truly successful.

One of my best-remembered meetings with such a man occurred on a little island called Cuttyhunk, off the Massachusetts coast. I had been strolling on the waterfront, and I paused to admire a gorgeous cruiser that was equipped for big-game fishing. The basic boat must have cost $200,000, and it was provided with a special fish-spotting platform, outriggers for trolling the bait, huge "fighting chairs" that hold you down when you hook into a 500-pounder, a device for sliding the monster into the cockpit, radar . . . the works.

Later I was invited aboard for a wonderful meal of fresh swordfish steak. The meal, complete with wines, was served by a steward. There were three others in the crew, including a maid for the owner's wife.

This couple spent six or eight months a year aboard their yacht, going north or south with the weather. Now and then the owner picked up the mike of his ship-to-shore phone and communicated with his office in Chicago. If there was an interesting opera in New York or Milan or a promising play in London, the couple would fly in from the Bahamas—or wherever they happened to be—to see it, and do some shopping. By way of an extra hobby, the owner took observations of currents, water temperatures, bottom profiles and so forth, and contributed his findings to an oceanographic institute. He called himself semiretired. He was filled both with energy and with a quiet contentment . . . a very special kind of happiness.

He hardly had to tell me that he had always known how he was going to spend the money he made (as distinguished from men who think of nothing but making money, and never really find out what they want to buy with it.) This man had started with nothing but a failing, debt-ridden family enterprise that he'd been strongly advised to put into bankruptcy. He'd made the business pay. And *pay*. Not for the prime reason of earning money, but for the prime reason of buying the finest kind of big-game fishing cruiser and the privilege of sailing north and south with the seasons and flying off to see a show when he wished. He said the fact that his goal was warm and personal made him achieve the goal. He guided himself with the one key question: *Will this help me go where I want to go?* —and he got there.

I have dined with richer men on yachts that required a crew of twenty. Not one of them was as downright *successful* as that man who had defined his dream, worked for it and won it.

"There is no substitute for money," he said that quiet afternoon, "but money is a means, not an end. It's a tool, you might say. If you want to build a house, you have to have the right tools. But, if you get more interested in the tools than in the house, you're way off the track. Money isn't what you want to get done; it's what gets something done for you. You want it so that you can exchange it for something you *really* want." He poured me a glass of a magnificent liqueur rum he'd picked up in Barbados. "When money buys you what you *want,* you have bought something that really can't be measured in money."

"Do you agree that when a man knows what he wants, something goes to work inside him that makes him more able to get it?"

"Absolutely! It's like magic."

It's very pleasant to have someone agree with you! But what that well-heeled vagabond and I agreed upon one day in Cuttyhunk is nothing but an ancient truth about human nature:

Once you have a definite goal in mind—a goal that comes out of your own deep desires and the inward recesses of your personality —mighty forces come to your aid. Those forces help you make your dream come true. That's the way it works! The money you need to achieve your goal, the ability, whatever you may need to achieve your dearest dream now comes within your reach.

Why is this so? Emerson spoke well when he said: "The world makes way for a man who knows where he is going." Such is the mystique of the human spirit that, when you deeply know what you want, you set up a kind of mental framework to fill in. You then automatically adjust your life to fill that framework. And this great focusing of your efforts is the surest way to double, triple and quadruple all the mighty dynamics of your will to win.

Money is only a means toward an end.

You may ask, "What's wrong with saying: 'My goal is to make a million dollars'?" My answer is: The only thing wrong with making a million dollars is calling it a goal. It's a step *toward* a goal, in its healthier aspect. Except to the miser, there is nothing warm and personal about money. Many a man focuses on nothing but money in the expectation of making his pile and then deciding how he'll have a rip-roaring good time with it. Suddenly, sitting on his moneybags, he is faced with the question, *Now what?*—and can only borrow someone else's answer.

I know a man who made a fortune and then asked a friend what he could do with the spare time he now had. The friend said: "See Europe!" So the man took his wife expensively to Europe. After a month of seeing Europe, the wife decided she'd never wanted to travel after all, and went home. The man stuck it out another month, then came home too, very gloomy. As Charles Kettering said: "Success is getting what you want; happiness is wanting what you get."

So you want a million dollars? No, my friend, say rather that you want what the million will buy for you—*and decide what it is*. Then you are much more likely to make your million *and* enjoy spending it.

Sometimes, though, taking a man's mind away from a goal of nothing-but-money is like rescuing a fly from flypaper. At one time —until my insurance agent begged me to stop—I had a rescue system that worked moderately well. I kept a batch of thousand-dollar bills in my desk drawer. When I was counseling some individual with a low income and he said, "Never mind goals; just give me the million and I'll find what to do with it," I would scatter those beautiful green G's across the desk, right under his nose. Then I would challenge him to tell me *instantly* what goal they might help him attain. *Instantly*, I insisted.

Some men grew angry.

Some men stammered and hesitated, and I cut them off. If they didn't know instantly, they didn't know. (Then *they* grew angry.)

Some, however, were made silent and thoughtful by my twenty-thousand-dollar shock treatment. I made headway with some of these men. And of that group, a number have come back to tell me that their success and happiness began the day they focused on a warm, living, personal goal that might depend on money but was not money itself.

Can you do that? Decide what you want your money to buy for you?

TA: PART ONE: DECIDE WHAT YOU WANT YOUR MONEY TO BUY FOR YOU.

What is *your* dearest dream? You are limited only to dreams that money can make come true. And hang the cost. Make it BIG. Small dreams do not have the power to stir you. Nor should you hedge your goal with fussy considerations of "worthiness." Since you are a social being, and unlikely to retire to a private satellite, I daresay you will keep your goal within the bounds of the law. But within those bounds you can be quite individualistic—and in all events make sure your goal is YOURS. You may indeed share a goal's benefits with your spouse or children or others—but still, make sure that YOUR goal is YOUR goal. You want to take charge of *your* goal-winning power—put it to work with thunderbolt energy—and you cannot do that with a borrowed goal. Your goal must be uniquely your own; then, building on that dearest dream, you build a goal-winning power that sweeps everything before it.

Stop and decide on a truly terrific long-term goal, perhaps for your retirement years; or, better, for semiretirement, or whatever suits your personal setup. I repeat: make it BIG. Don't hem it in. Is it a goal of personal power? A goal of social service? A goal of adventure? A goal built on your hobby? A combination of these? Whatever it may be, give it wings! Let it sing!

Write it here in big capital letters:

MY GOLDEN GOAL IS _____

And that is the first part of your Teleological Action for this chapter. It may take you awhile to fill in that blank, but when you have done so, go straight into Teleological Action: Part Two. This next Action actually gets you going toward your goal, yes, actually gets you off and running. And if you have chosen a goal that is not right for *you*, you'll be quickly led to a better, stronger choice.

TA: PART TWO: SET UP A GOLDEN GOAL FILE.

This file can be set up in anything that holds papers. Preferably it should be set up in a box or a file drawer of the correct size to hold papers upright for easy reference. A shoebox is too small. You need something big enough to hold the entire big picture of your Golden Goal.

For your first entry in your Golden Goal File, take a clean sheet of paper and print in big letters the description of your Golden Goal. A few words will do. The following are adapted from real choices:

> Build and live in the house of my dreams.
> Live in the locale of my dreams.
> Set up a great scientific or sociological foundation to
>   make the world a better place to live in.
> A dream fishing yacht stocked with dream equipment.
> A grand photography expedition (with dream equip-
>   ment) to the national parks. (Tibet. Antarctica.)

Become the world's greatest authority on dahlias. (The Vikings. Etruscan pottery. Language structure.)

Finance and run a chain of clubs where young people can meet in pleasant surroundings.

Build my church into a position of greatness.

Travel to (any place that interests you).

Get all the equipment I need to work on several ideas for inventions.

Go back to where my education left off and get a Ph.D. in (you name it).

Learn to sing. (Paint. Play some musical instrument well enough to be admired.)

Become mayor of my town. (President of the United States.)

None of these may be precisely *your* Golden Goal, but let's take a couple of them as instances. Let's see how a Golden Goal File does its work.

You now have your Golden Goal in mind and in writing. Let's say it is: *I want to build and live in the house of my dreams.* Your first file entry is taken care of. Now look for and file all kinds of auxiliary information, any information which makes your purpose more real and easy to picture, relates it to your present life, helps you to perfect it, to fill in its details, to extend it into the several areas of your life. For example:

> *I want to build and live in the house of my dreams.*
> [Your Golden Goal File will get fat with pictures of houses and parts of houses, interior decorating schemes, color charts, data on paint, landscaping layouts. You may add plans and ideas for a woodworking shop over the garage, or a greenhouse at the rear, or a pottery kiln at the foot of the garden. You'll have data on ideal locations for your gorgeous home. What with furnishings, built-ins, entertaining arrangements and so forth, your dream will extend your interests and plans in a dozen different directions.]

Let's take another. *Travel* seems to be on everybody's mind.

40

You may say: "I'll get a globe, whirl it around and throw a dart at it. Wherever the dart sticks, that's where I'll go." Fine! Or you may do it in other ways, of which I'll indicate a few:

I want to travel.

[Having decided where to go, for your own reasons, you'd get brochures or other information on the place or places. Probably you'd find interest in certain specialties such as clothing, or odd folkways, and this kind of data would also go into your Golden Goal File. Seeing yourself and/or your companion and/or your group traveling by ship or plane, later by sampan or donkey or camel, you'd file information on clothing and equipment you'd need. (A hobby of photography or painting would work in nicely.) Your interest being, say, in cathedrals, you could lay out a leisurely, first-class cathedral tour and let the country be incidental to its cathedrals. A leisurely ancestor-tour, with plenty of money for souvenirs, would bring you to the town or farm where your forebears lived in the Old Country. Your branching interests could lead you into a study of the needed language or languages. And so forth.]

Keep your Golden Goal File active.

Go through your Golden Goal File at least once a week, weeding out some material as you gain more sophisticated knowledge, adding new material, checking forward, checking back.

More than this: *Live* a little while with the picture of your Golden Goal as it grows under your eyes. What used to be a mere idea is now taking on solid proportions. How does it sit with you now?

At this point—and it will come very soon after you start your Golden Goal File—you may realize you borrowed someone else's goal. Perhaps you were so anxious to have a Golden Goal that you grabbed at the first suggestion. Very well! Far from no-harm-done, be assured that a great deal of *good* has been done. You took a wrong turn, but you stopped before you got lost. And now all your sense of purpose and your take-charge powers are alerted. Your mistake has made you stronger, wiser, more confident than you were before—and your Golden Goal File did this for you.

So, if you see you chose the wrong goal, clean out your file and wait for your great, new, true goal to filter up into your wide-awake consciousness. This will not take long. Probably your subconscious mind is making you act it out in some manner, and one day—presto!—you'll see the pattern. The man I met at Cuttyhunk told me he hadn't realized what impelled him to visit the Motor Boat Show every year, until suddenly he realized he was acting out what he wanted.

Of course your first choice of goal may be *it*. This happens more than half the time to younger men, I would estimate, and 90 per cent of the time to men who have put some experience behind them.

That the life's goal is found is not nearly so amazing as the *effect* when it is found. The man who finds his goal has found a very deep and special expression of *himself*, and the effect is tremendous. It may be that for another quarter-century he will seem to be living the ordinary life of work, play and sleep, but it is no longer ordinary. His very enjoyment of each day is quickened by the knowledge of where he is going. Upward steps in career, increases of income, now are far more significant because they represent progress toward the goal, which is goal-gaining power.

The man who finds his Golden Goal is more alive. He is better organized. And above all, he has a grand framework for his life's efforts. He asks himself: *Will this take me where I want to go?*— and in the very asking he keeps himself on the road, looking ahead, moving.

Your Golden Goal File can give you immediate money benefit.

Here sits a salesman in his unhappy home, watching TV. All day he sells, or tries to sell, a very good loose-leaf service for accountants. Four hours every evening, he watches TV. Other salesmen who handle the same loose-leaf service take an evening now and then to keep themselves up to date on new tax rules and regulations, so that they can "talk the customer's language." But our friend lacks something he calls energy. He claims it takes a full evening of TV, every evening, to restore his strength for next day's struggle.

Our paths crossed and we had a chat. He began: "If only I had enough money . . ." but even that didn't sound convincing. When I asked him if he had ever visualized himself as being fulfilled and happy in a certain role, he waved the idea away. At last he did confess to a long-submerged dream of being a gentleman farmer. Fat chance! He was barely keeping up the payments on his TV set.

"Well, how about setting up a Golden Goal File? You'd certainly find it interesting to collect information on soils, crops, labor-saving devices that have revolutionized farming, breeds of cattle—"

"Oh no. It's too late. I'm fifty-one."

"The only thing that fifty-one is too late for is celebrating your fiftieth birthday."

He sat there looking haunted. At last he spoke, like a child who is not making good marks and says he *wants* to fail in school. "Aw, I don't really want to be a gentleman farmer."

"Still, the idea has stayed with you about twenty years." And I went on talking about it. I suggested a home of modern sun-roof construction and that got a flash of interest out of him. No, he said, he had dreamed of a traditional model farmhouse built of field-stone. Again he turned gloomy. I steered the conversation to the interaction of *act, think* and *feel* in the human personality. I suggested that no matter how he thought and felt, the mere *action* of setting up a Golden Goal File could do something for him. He shrugged and went away.

Six months later, he started that file. That was a year and a half ago. He suddenly found he *could* do his necessary homework because it was going to help him become a gentleman farmer. And he went out selling forcefully and convincingly because it was going to help him toward his Golden Goal.

Concurrently he found out what many other lethargic people ought to find out—that expending energy builds more energy. His income has more than doubled, and it is constantly climbing. He is being considered as a district manager. He breaks away from that TV set to take out his wife, and they are much friendlier than they used to be. His waistline has come in two inches. His health—so often a reflection of the *spirit* rather than the *body*—has greatly improved. And his enthusiastic speech at a salesman's meeting got three others started on their Golden Goal Files.

You also take charge of your interim goals.

We may look at successful people and see no indication of the many steps they took in climbing to the top. But a Golden Goal builds upon many steps climbed, many interim goals achieved, new goals set up, and those achieved as well, until the Golden Goal is attained.

It is the great Golden Goal that constantly reinvigorates your goal-winning power. Otherwise you'd hardly know an interim goal from a stopping place. Many a man never discovers a quarter of his full potential—in money, in achievement or in happiness—because he stops short . . . because he never really knew where he was going.

TA: PART THREE: SET UP AN INTERIM GOAL FILE.

Your interim goals still are *your* goals and should reflect your own inward drives and talents. But where your Golden Goal is likely to stand as a money-*spending* experience, your interim goals will be more concerned with activities that *earn* money, the money that brings your Golden Goal alive.

Set up your Interim Goal File in essentially the same way as your Golden Goal File, although you may want to have several sections in it for several interim goals. Shift and change as you see fit. It is here that you'll keep asking yourself that highly important question: *Will this take me where I want to go?*

A favorite interim goal for a good many men is: *I want to start and build a business of my own.* Suppose this were your own interim goal, and that after sufficient thought and experience you have decided what kind of business it is going to be, but you must delay a year or more before you can leave your present job and get started. Your Interim Goal File would shape up something like this:

> *I want to start and build a business of my own.*
> [You'll have up-to-date figures on the trends and patterns of your business. You'll have newspaper clippings that deal with any governmental activity which

may concern it, and also dozens of "how-to" clippings from trade magazines. You'll have file folders full of information on the wholesale sources of goods you want to sell, or sources of the materials you wish to process into salable goods; or sources of the equipment you'll need for any service you wish to render. You'll also keep an up-to-date sketch file of factory or office layouts, and information on possible factory or office sites. You may be able to join a trade organization in your line. Where you may need some special skill or other know-how, you'll know about it and you'll have it under your belt by the time you need it. Your file also can guide you in a number of "dry runs" of your business routine; you can set up a trial budget, an organization chart, a plan for expansion.]

As with your Golden Goal File, keep this file alive. Go through it once a week. Add new, exciting data; weed out deadwood. It is when you *live* your goal that it comes alive!

The goal of one man I knew was to expand his commercial refrigeration business and make it the biggest one in his state. He ran into difficulty because of certain political pressures, and he was stymied. But in going through his Interim Goal File one evening, he came upon an item he had clipped about climatic influences on refrigeration. He had also been reading about the way some sleepy West Indian islands have been booming lately—and *because he had a stirred-up sense of GOAL* his mind took charge of those two items and saw the connection between them. A quick flight down the line of Caribbean islands showed him three towns that needed commercial refrigeration plants; he landed contracts for two of these, has branched into supplying them with frozen foods, and, as he says, he is now swinging.

Once you know your goals, your mind delivers goal-winning ideas. Your mind makes meaningful patterns out of events and incidents and bits of data which, if you did not have a mental frame of reference, might be meaningless to you. You cannot know how strongly and wonderfully this mind-magic works until you set up a Golden Goal File and an Interim Goal File to constantly build and broaden your goal-winning power.

45

TA: PART FOUR: X-RAY YOUR FAVORITE "HANDICAP" AND SEE IF IT ISN'T A LOSER'S LIMP.

"Watch this," chuckled an athletic coach as we watched his track team compete in a high-school athletic meet. "You see my boy coming in fourth, there? Limping? Chances are he just developed that limp to have an excuse for not doing better. I call it loser's limp."

Some of the reasons why some men do not attain their goals—do not get one-tenth of the way to their goals—are no more convincing than the high-school boy's suddenly developed limp. Worse yet, the loser's-limp attitude may stop a man from even trying to lift his life above a subsistence level. When the gun goes off to start the race, he is licked before he starts.

He may put it to you earnestly: "You can see how badly I am handicapped by . . ." and what follows is something defined as a handicap. Very rarely is it actually a handicap. Over and over, when some man tells me he is handicapped, I see a built-in loser's limp.

I am not talking about blind people, although one can still learn a wonderful lesson from Helen Keller. I am not talking about bedridden people, notwithstanding the fact that such men as James Royce, completely immobilized by polio, have built a thriving business from their beds. We should take off our hats to *really* handicapped people who still live constructive lives, but they are too exceptional for most of us to identify with.

I am talking, rather, about men who have the use of all their senses and all their limbs, surely the great majority of my readers.

And perhaps I speak directly to YOU—if you have never taken charge of your life-dynamics; if you know that many and many another man, who has nothing you haven't got, is building a grand career and a glorious future while *you* get pushed into some low-level corner. If you've lost a few of life's races, see if you're not *assuming* you're a loser forever, if you're not acquiring a loser's limp before you start.

Check yourself for loser's limp right now! But remember, as you check the "handicaps" you encounter, that they may not be handicaps at all. In fact you may have one of the three most popular loser's limps.

46

1. I am handicapped by lack of sufficient education.

"Education?" said a top-ranking man in a big business-machine company. "Every now and then we promote some school-of-hard-knocks fellow right over the head of someone who owns a string of degrees. Then we tell the fellow with the degrees to stop leaning on them and get to work."

"Education?" said a personnel manager. "Sure, we have a place for education on our application blank. But when I find a man who believes in himself and who has enthusiasm for the job he wants to fill, and doesn't have much education, I give him a waiver on education. Find me enough enthusiastic, hard-working men who want to go somewhere and I'll black out the question on education."

True enough, some jobs can't be held if you don't have certain degrees. But there are millions of good jobs, big-pay jobs, jobs with rich futures you can hold without ever going to college. Harry Truman never went to college. Henry Ford never went to college. Thomas Edison not only had no advanced education, but was despaired of by his grade-school teachers. W. Clement Stone, the Chicago insurance executive, is a high-school drop-out who ran a capital of one hundred dollars into hundreds of millions of dollars.

Men who complain to me about their lack of education are likely to get their noses rubbed in a quotation from Thomas Paine: "As to the learning that any person gains from school education, it serves only like a small capital, to put him in the way of beginning learning for himself afterwards. Every person . . . is finally his own teacher."

Your will to win, your willingness to take charge of your life and make something good of it, your *un*willingness to compare loser's limps with the rest of the bellyachers . . . these are what make you happy and wealthy and successful. *You always have what it takes to be successful.* And because every person *is* finally his own teacher, never confuse education with knowledge.

Knowledge is power.

And knowledge specifically relevant to your goal is terrific power. I am thinking of a youngish man who told me, on a Monday, that on the coming Wednesday he was to be interviewed for a public rela-

47

tions job. He wanted the job, but the company wanted a man who'd had experience in their field. He didn't have a bit of experience in the field. What could he do?

I told him to spend the rest of the day in the library, reading all the trade magazines in that field and making notes to study during the evening.

On Tuesday I sent him to a large department store that sold the product in question, a household appliance. He was to "shop" like a very cautious customer, note the features of the appliance and how they were "sold" to him. Then he was to go to other stores and do the same for competing products. Then he was to return to the library, inspect a register of corporations and find out the company's vital statistics and the names of its key men. Then go to *Who's Who* and get to know those men. He was also to see how the company's stock had been doing and to check other similar items. Meanwhile, I had procured a few copies of the company's house organ for him to look over.

P.S. He got the job. And he got it in perfect honesty, saying he had studied the subject only a few days.

He simply had specific knowledge that showed in his conversation with the interviewer. They saw in him the foundation for that very valuable person, the man who knows the answers, because he was now the man who knows he has to become the man who knows the answers.

And by the way: Their Help Wanted ad had said "college degree preferred," and this chap's education had stopped in the eighth grade.

Education *is* valuable. But lack of education is *not* a handicap unless you say it is.

Have you been using *lack of education* as a loser's limp?
Check here: (   ) Yes   (   ) No

2. *I am handicapped because I am simply not smart enough.*

When a man is too fond of his will to lose—or just too lazy—to acquire the knowledge he needs for success, he often limps into this special rut. "I just don't have the brains it takes to succeed," he says, and feels vindicated.

Man is superior to animals not only because he is more intelligent but also because he is better equipped to use his intelligence.

48

Brains depend for their effect largely on how they are used. To nail down that point, let us think about some relatively intelligent animal. The dolphin is a good example. Despite being fish-shaped, this warm-blooded mammal seems to be above average in learning ability, apparently has a social sense and even a kind of language. We are only just beginning to study the dolphin; some say that when we really get to know him, we shall find he is as intelligent as man.

All right, let us say that an average dolphin is, truly, as intelligent as an average man. But the dolphin lives in the sea, so he is forever limited by his environment. Shaped and equipped to make his way through water, he has no hands with which to develop or use tools, let alone that he can never master the use of fire. His language will never develop into anything like the human being's vast ability to communicate. If indeed he has some knowledge beyond what he needs in order to survive—and, as some say, a knowledge of how to help shipwrecked sailors—he still will never develop a body of recorded knowledge. For millions of generations, no dolphin generation has been more advanced in *opportunity to use its intelligence* than the generation before it. Now that we are training dolphins to perform such tasks as carrying messages (in human writing) from diver to diver, we only emphasize that fact.

Agree, if you will, that a dolphin is *potentially* as smart as a man, and you emphasize the fact that intelligence is nothing but a *potential*. Intelligence may be compared to a battery packed with latent power; but that power is not apparent until you hook up the battery to a motor or a light—and close the switch.

It is man who has the inestimable advantage of using his intelligence in countless ways: of focusing his intelligence so that it does its best for him, of receiving an endless flow of information he can sift for the facts that help him most, of living in surroundings that have been highly modified through his own efforts to afford more and more and more opportunity to be of profitable service. Comparing man with any other form of life, we may well exclaim with Shakespeare: "What a piece of work is man!"

And then man turns around and uses his amazing mind in order to defeat himself, which is what you do when you govern your life with a loser's limp. Especially when you say: "I am handicapped because I am not smart enough."

49

A very well placed executive told me: "Most of my assistants are more intelligent than I am. Some of them are so intelligent they never get anything done because they are so good at finding reasons why it can't be done."

There is a classic story of a group of engineers who were asked to develop a glass-to-metal bond in a tricky TV installation. They never tried. They merely submitted well-documented scientific reasons to show why it could not be done. Then a mere lab technician, not considered very bright, "fooled around" with the problem a couple of days and solved it.

Check among men who are doing well in business or in politics or even in education, and you'll rarely find an above-average intelligence quotient. What you *will* find among successful men everywhere is a good hook-up of available potential to the tasks they want to accomplish. Their brain-power is backed with a concentrated emotion-power, a Will to Win, a sense of Goal that brings an almost irresistible focus.

With the man who does not hook up his intelligence and *use* it, it is as though sunlight were falling upon a sheet of paper and scarcely warming the paper. If you really want to hook up that sunlight to a task, get a magnifying glass and focus the same amount of sunlight into a fiery dot, and the paper burns right through.

With all this talk about intelligence, perhaps you are wondering just what intelligence is, after all. Everybody wonders. I.Q. is only a clumsy way to measure *something*. *Intelligence* is very hard to define. But it is easy to demonstrate that you don't need any noteworthy amount of "brightness" or "sharpness" in order to be wealthy and happy. Just look around! Over and over you are going to observe, and, I hope, learn, one great lesson:

It's not the size of your intelligence that counts; it's the size of what you do with it.

Have you been using "I'm not smart enough" as your loser's limp? Check here: (   ) Yes   (   ) No

The third most popular loser's limp is really pitiful. Alas, it is also plentiful.

3. *I am handicapped because I never get the breaks.*
You can say this in several ways: "Other people have all the

50

luck," "Fate is against me" and so forth. If you say it *any* way, you are a victim of loser's limp. You have assumed your limp because you don't really want the breaks, you won't put yourself in a position to get the breaks, so you limpingly declare that you and good luck are out of step forever.

There is really no such thing as luck. There are chains of events, one thing leading to another. When it comes to circumstances in which we have no way to affect or predict the chain of events—for example, the chain of events that might lead you to pick a winning sweepstakes number—the word *luck* does have some meaning. But as you know, this is distinctly the exception!

The RULE is: *You make your own breaks; you create your own "luck."*

How? By announcing, as it were, that you keep an open house for *lucky breaks* and inviting them to visit. And by what process do you keep open-house so that a lucky break, wandering by, will drop in? By really *working* at your job with all the concentration and determination and concrete useful knowledge and goal-winning drive you can muster.

A printer, referring to his competitor, complained: "Look at the break Adams got! When *XY* magazine needed a rush job on a special four-color insert, they phoned him first and he got the job. If they'd phoned me, I'd have shown them I'm as well equipped as he is, and I'd have gotten the job. I suppose they just phoned the first name they found listed under "Printers.' "

No, they hadn't. But Adams had joined a publishers' association and had made himself known as a first-class four-color printer.

An experienced salesman made three calls on a restaurant that really needed new coffee urns and other equipment, but he couldn't make a sale. A new man walked into the same restaurant, and "found them in a mood to buy," the experienced salesman said in disgust. Not at all. The new man took charge of the chain of events, and wrote a big order, because he had figures that showed to the penny how new equipment could pay for itself.

Later we shall set up Teleological Actions that add progress and profit and goal-gaining power to any job you do. Meanwhile, take a grip on this well-proven maxim: *There is always a way to WORK THROUGH YOUR JOB and create great breaks that carry you ahead*. Use these questions to guide you:

51

HOW can I extend the breadth and scope of my job, give it added values?

WHAT specific knowledge will be useful in doing this?

WHO should know more about me and the services I render?

I specify *work through your job* to get your mind attuned to chains of events you can swing your way—and to get your mind *off* sweepstakes and daily doubles. Your job, *any* job, has so many opportunities to MAKE YOUR OWN LUCKY BREAKS that when you really want those breaks you'll see how to make them.

This hardly exhausts the subject, and this book will recount many more true stories of people who made their own breaks instead of avoiding the issue.

Have you been using "I never get the breaks" as your loser's limp? Check here: (   ) Yes   (   ) No

And so, having surveyed three major roadblocks that men erect in their own minds, let us reaccentuate the positive.

Goal power is life power.

Literally, figuratively, in every possible way it can be meant, *goal power is life power*.

In its most literal sense, the relation of the sense of goal to the body's vital forces is something that has not yet been explained. But it is there, a power beyond logic.

A man was told he was dying of cancer. He said he wanted to live to see his motherless son, then ten years old, reach his twenty-first birthday. The doctors unanimously shook their heads; one gave him three months to live; one said he might last six months. But that "dying" man set a goal: He would see his son reach twenty-one. In the next few weeks the radiation treatments seemed to hold the cancer in check when before they had not. Later he got out of bed and did some useful work, so he was given another six months to live. And another six months. And another . . . till at length he died of cancer a few weeks after his son's twenty-first birthday.

A prospector was stranded in an Australian desert when his jeep broke down. He had to walk to the foot of a distant peak where he could find water. His feet blistered, his tongue swelled in his parched mouth, but he kept going by setting up one goal after another . . . "I'll reach that rock" . . . "I'll crawl to that clump of cactus." Goal by goal he built toward his ultimate goal, and he reached it. A sheep rancher who found him at the water hole told him flatly that his story was impossible; nobody could have survived that trek on foot, without water.

You may demur that goals of this kind are *physical* goals as distinguished from goals of mental endeavor. But the similarities among all kinds of goals are far stronger than their differences. The physical goal is achieved on the basis of a prior mental image of the goal. The mental image supplied the extra impulse that broke the four-minute mile. It got men to the top of Mount Everest. And always, with any goal of any kind at any time, the more vividly you see your goal and the more you feel it and truly live it in anticipation, the more sure you are of getting there.

Goal-power is life-power of a kind that cannot adequately be described. When you find it, you know it. And how you enjoy it! Working for you constantly as you build the career and the fortune that result in living your dearest dream, goal-power becomes a sparkling central dynamo of life-power and power for life.

I remind you again that *the way you act is the way you think is the way you feel is the way you act—is the way you LIVE.*

The tested key that starts the great cycle going is *Teleological Action.*

Where we have been:

It's good to have money, but money can let you down when it does not buy you something that is warm and meaningful to you. The deeply felt goal toward which you work is a great aid in making the money you need to get there. When money has bought you something you really want, you have bought something that cannot be measured in money.

Decide what you want your money to buy for you. Write it in big capital letters. Start a Golden Goal File, and file all kinds of information about the goal of your dreams . . . anything that helps you perfect it, anything that helps you extend it into several areas of your life.

Your Golden Goal File helps you *live* your goal. It gives you energy, drive and enthusiasm and so can result in immediate money benefit. You also take charge of your interim goals and set up an Interim Goal File which keeps you constantly organized toward the activities that earn your money. Once you know your goals, your mind combines facts and circumstances into great goal-winning ideas.

Don't surrender your goals to *loser's limp*! If you think you are handicapped by lack of education, remember that specific knowledge is what counts. If you think you are not smart enough to succeed, remember it's not the size of your intelligence that counts, it's the size of what you do with it. If you think you get "bad breaks," look at all the evidence that shows we make our own breaks, create our own good luck. Goal-power is life-power, dynamic and victorious.

Where we are going:

In the next chapter we do justice to the fact that your day-by-day success often depends upon the way you handle people. Key secrets of human nature will now be ready in your mind, and you will find them of tremendous power.

4 Master Other People's Minds

You can control and influence others in many important ways, not by arguing with them, but through the truly effective art of working through their emotions. You can get other people actually to WANT to do what you want them to do. A few key Teleological Actions quickly give you the main levers of control, and you can go ahead to win the benefit of your new take-charge power with your family, friends, customers—anyone you wish.

"Now let *me* tell *you* a human-nature story," the company's consulting psychiatrist said across our chessboard.

"It's your turn to tell one," I agreed.

"Well, there was this fellow named Green. He was a fairly ordinary neurotic—"

"Just what does that mean?"

The psychiatrist sighed. "Well, as we say in the trade, a normal person knows that two and two make four. A psychotic—that is, an insane person—knows that two and two make five. A neurotic knows that two and two make four, but he can't quite accept the fact. An ordinary neurotic is largely occupied with his distorted view of life and in making difficulties for himself. Now, can we get back to my man Green?

"He was not too badly off, but he decided his case was unique. In fact, that was part of his neurosis. He decided he was so uniquely afflicted that only a very special psychiatrist could help him. One by one he became a patient of nearly every psychiatrist in the city, but nobody he tried seemed special enough.

"By the time Green got around to me, I had heard about him.

When he let me know I was to have the privilege of treating him, I decided to give him a pretreatment before he ever entered my office. I was going to work through his emotional self-interest and make him see me as somebody who must be *very* special.

"So, when he phoned for an appointment, I gave him a date four weeks ahead and told him I was much too busy to see him any sooner. He took that hard. He said he would go mad if he couldn't see me right away. I knew he would not go mad, repeated the date and the hour I would see him, and hung up.

"In those four weeks, Green called me a dozen times. Sometimes he called me at 2:00 A.M. to tell me how desperate he was to see me. I went on playing hard-to-get, pretreating him, making him more and more sure I must be very, very special. Soon he was telling me he *knew* I was the only one who could get him out of his mess. He even got his wife, poor woman, to intercede for him, but I went on playing hard-to-get.

"When that man finally entered my office he had tremendous faith in me. By working on his emotional self-interest I had almost worked a faith cure before he ever saw me. When I got him on my couch, I didn't *do* anything for him that my colleagues could not have done, but he's in good shape now."

"That's a wonderful story," I said. "Does that kind of appeal work only with neurotics?"

"Shucks, no. It works with everybody. Playing hard-to-get is just one way of doing it."

"Yes, I can see that. But if you want someone to believe you're pretty special—to take charge of his mind so that he is going to believe in you and your abilities—it's a good idea to play hard-to-get?"

"That's right, if the occasion warrants it." The psychiatrist paused and looked far beyond me. "You know . . ." he said, "I just realized . . . that's what Isobel did to me."

"Isobel. Your wife? She played hard-to-get?"

"Yes. I just realized it—and we've been married thirty years!"

To take charge of someone else's mind, work through his emotional self-interest.

Emotional self-interest can be defined as something that benefits you *and* something that pleases you. Logic has its place—second place. But work on the other fellow's emotions, *and* work on the other fellow's self-interest to get him to go the way you want him to go. You may change his mind permanently or it may be for just a moment, but enough of those magic take-charge moments make a tremendous difference in your success!

The key word in the phrase is "emotional." Take the example of a teacher who pleads with her class to try for higher marks in their own self-interest for the sake of their future. Not sufficiently emotional; no results. Then she sets up a bulletin board headed VERY IMPORTANT PEOPLE and posts the names and averages of those who are doing well. She asks those who are failing if they too wouldn't enjoy being up there with the VERY IMPORTANT PEOPLE. She thus digs at the universal emotional *need to be recognized*—and the class average goes up 18 per cent.

A night watchman on the New York water front sees a woman about to jump off a deserted pier. "Come near and I'll jump!" she screams. The watchman calls her attention to the oil, the floating garbage and the dead cat in the water—and suddenly she cannot bear to jump into that nasty stuff. Weeping, she allows him to lead her off. She probably wanted subconsciously to be stopped from suicide, but surely no *logical* reason would have stopped her. Indeed, people often *prefer* to set logic aside and find emotional reasons for their actions. We seem to feel we are better understood, better appreciated when we do.

In fact, we tend more often to agree with each other on an emotional rather than on a logical level. For example: A salesman entered a hotel in Abilene and said to the desk clerk. "Give me a good room. At the commercial rate, of course." Meaning, he expected to be accommodated overnight at a reduced rate.

The clerk had no logical reason to reduce the room rate. But he felt impelled to do it. (It was expected of him!) So he put the entire matter onto an emotional level—a between-us-friends level. "Sure!" he said. "I wouldn't do it for some fella from 'way off somewhere, but I'm glad to make a rate for one of our own Kansas boys." And that is how the salesman from Cincinnati, Ohio, saved a couple of dollars.

The self-interest, here, lay in the clerk's assuming a camaraderie that made him feel like a "regular fella." The salesman probably didn't plan it that way, but the rule still worked. *When you approach another person through his EMOTIONAL SELF–INTEREST, that person WANTS to do what you want him to do.*

Now let us go into Teleological Action that sets up emotional self-interest as a mighty tool of influence and control over others.

TA: PART ONE: EXAMINE YOUR OWN EMOTIONAL SELF–INTEREST.

The following quiz is set up to put you "in the shoes" of each person described in the left-hand column. Imagine yourself to be that person. Then go to the right-hand column and put a check mark next to the appeal you believe would be most effective in "selling" that person. Don't hesitate to use big, black check marks. This is *your* book, and the more you make it yours personally, the more it will help you take charge of a bigger, better, brighter life.

Also, the various instances here and elsewhere will remind you of similar instances in your own life. Jot them down right in the book. Years from now you'll come back to this book, and you will see how you have changed and learned in the years between.

Now for the quiz on emotional self-interest:

If you were	You would respond more readily to (check one)
A man interested in buying a retail business	( ) This business performs a needed service to the community.
	( ) This business will return 50 per cent of your investment the first year.
The father of a fourth grader	( ) Sir, this teaching machine was prepared by a committee of leading educators.
	( ) How would you like little Johnny to improve his reading 100 per cent in three days, and get rid of his spelling troubles?

58

A person wondering if he ought to sign up for an annuity	( )	You should be willing to deprive yourself of a little now in order to enjoy an income after you stop working.
	( )	You can retire at sixty-five with $500 a month guaranteed for life.
A fourteen-year-old bothered by facial eruptions	( )	This cream passed every laboratory test.
	( )	This cream clears up your blemishes in half an hour.
A man in his best suit, standing too close to a mechanic who is performing emergency repairs to his car. The mechanic says:	( )	I wish you'd give me more room to work in.
	( )	Watch out! You'll get grease on your pants!
The left end of a losing football team, listening to your coach between halves. The coach says:	( )	Win or lose, you'll still get your education at Old Siwash.
	( )	Tonight at that big dance you're going to be the heroes of Old Siwash, surrounded by girls, your names emblazoned forever in glory because you came from behind and won! Now get in there and fight!

Did you check the second appeal in each case? Most likely you did, since these represented emotional appeals to self-interest, while the first appeals were those of cool logic. I hope you judged the appeals from the point of view of the man who wanted to buy a retail business, the father of a fourth grader and so forth. It is very important to put yourself in the other fellow's shoes in order to understand him. And it is most important to do this when you want to reach into his mind and take charge of his thinking.

Now let us nail down the appeals with a bit of analysis.

The man interested in the store wants to make money. Sounds "practical" and "logical," doesn't it? Believe me, there is more emotion than logic connected with money! If this were not so, the Bible would not have warned that the *love* of money is the root of all evil; nor would we have people piling up more money than they can spend, and so busy doing it that they get no fun out of life. Besides all this, consider how strongly money is connected with our emotional needs for security, status, personal effectiveness . . . and fun as well.

The father of the fourth grader, like any parent, tends emotionally to live his child's life. He is gratified by his child's progress. It makes him "feel good."

The annuity purchaser wants a feeling of security, an emotion dear to all of us.

The fourteen-year-old also wants security of a sort, the security of looking his best and knowing he won't be avoided or sneered at.

The man in his best suit wishes to look well groomed as much as he wants to avoid grease stains and thus save on cleaning bills. (Anytime you save money you feel more secure.)

As for the left end, he'll break an arm for dear Old Siwash for the sake of recognition by the girls at the dance.

You can see the self-interest in each case. Behind each of these appeals to self-interest lies an emotion. By recognizing these basic human emotions, you can more easily direct your own appeals to them when you want to influence other people.

These emotions can be divided into five categories, and you can remember them by recalling the word ASHES:

ACQUISITIVENESS. People want money and they want what money buys.

SEX. We are sexual creatures and like to be reminded of it, and of the objectives of love and romance (and the many adornments related to them).

HEALTH. We all want to be and remain healthy.

EMULATION. We want to live up to standards, some set by the Joneses, some set by ourselves, all usually related to status.

SELF-PRESERVATION. We prefer to stay alive.

The negative side of each of these positive emotions is its corresponding *fear*. Fear can creep in everywhere, and if you make it

60

too welcome in your personality, pretty soon all you have left is the *fear* of not having enough money, the *fear* of sexual-romantic ineffectiveness, the *fear* of ill-health, the *fear* of lack of status, and the *fear* of death. So much depends on the attitude you take toward any emotion!

The annuity buyer, for example, wants money to come in at a time when he'll no longer be working; also, he is motivated by a fear of being destitute in his old age. Read any annuity ad and you are sure to find this fear worked on somewhere, albeit in good taste. Notice, however, that a good advertising writer—which means a good practical psychologist—rarely mentions a fear without telling you he is going to replace that fear (often meaning a lack or a feared lack) with a desirable benefit. For example:

YOU GET RID OF MONEY WORRIES WHEN YOU FOLLOW THIS SIMPLE PLAN.

GOT A HEADACHE? TAKE X ASPIRIN.

HOW I RAISED MYSELF FROM FAILURE TO SUCCESS.

The same negative-positive spirit will be followed in the small print. As one ad man told me, you don't have to bear down on fears. Just hint at them, and people will find their own.

In taking charge of other people's minds, accentuate the positive.

Save the outright fear-appeal for emergencies. You can almost always sway people by showing them some way to fulfill themselves. You don't have to tell them they have unfulfilled areas; they know it. Just show them a way to become bigger and better, richer, handsomer, more powerful, more secure, more desired, more admired, more important. Of these promises, *more important* is something of a catchall. *Status* means a great deal to everyone and it is a subtle thing. Even the hotel clerk, back there, was seeking a status of a sort.

TA: PART TWO: CHECK THE WAY A GOOD ADVERTISEMENT APPEALS TO YOUR EMOTIONAL SELF–INTEREST.

I leave it to you to find a good advertisement, or several, in your newspaper or any popular magazine. Don't be misled by flashy ads.

Good ads have to prove themselves, and, by and large, mail-order ads—the kind that tell you to send a coupon or write for a booklet —are the only ones that can really prove their success by the number of orders or requests that come in. When you see a mail-order ad that has been repeated over and over, read it carefully and think about it. Write down the number of ways in which it appeals to your (or to its logical customer's) emotional self-interest. You will learn something about swaying minds. And don't sneer at the obvious selling techniques. We all "sell" ourselves in one way or another.

I'll point out just two techniques that have proved to be very powerful.

1. "You'll be the envy of your neighborhood."

This works for Cadillacs (in a distinctly unsaid but *felt* way) as well as it works for $19.95 coffee tables. Note how items of the latter nature are often pictured being *admired* . . . which neatly raises the status of the lady who bought the item.

2. "Do me a favor."

Just what goes to work when you say to anyone else: "Do me a favor"? His desire to be big, important, noticed, invaluable. He doesn't stop to reason it out, but there it is!

This way of taking charge of other people's minds was used with great effect by Robert Collier, an old-time mail-order expert. When no one else could write an advertising letter that sold doctors' bags, Collier wrote one that began, "Will you do me a favor?" He followed by saying the favor was easy and pleasant to do and cost nothing. By now the reader was powerfully impelled to read the rest of the message—and once you begin to pay attention, you begin to be committed.

Now, the favor was merely to look over the beautifully described and obviously useful bag on a free trial basis. By the time the reader got that far, however, he had been pretty well sold on possessing the thing *in his own self-interest*. Thousands of doctors bought bags because of that letter.

As long as *do me a favor* is not overdone, people like you if you ask them for a favor!

I am thinking of a man who bought a house next to a surly,

uncooperative neighbor—or so the neighbor had been described to him. Still, when the new homeowner had difficulty in hanging a mirror on a hard cinder-block wall, he asked the "surly" neighbor for assistance. And the neighbor came with his electric drill and his masonry bit and practically did the whole job. The new homeowner had merely said: "Say, you've been through all this mess, so maybe you can tell me what I'm doing wrong. How in the world can you hang a mirror where you can't even drive a nail?"

Appeal to a man in the area of his special competence, and how he loves you! You make him so BIG!

For that matter, people will go out of their way to do a favor even when it is not requested, provided it can make them feel in some way superior. A taxi driver told me he is always willing to change a tire for any male motorist—for one buck. But he will volunteer to change a tire for any stranded lady motorist, and will refuse payment. "It makes me feel good to do a favor for anyone who really is helpless," he said.

TA: PART THREE: KNOW AND USE THESE OTHER POWERFUL HUMAN–NATURE LEVERS.

A lever moves large weights with the application of a relatively small force. A human-nature lever moves people's minds, sometimes with the application of so small a force, it is shocking. I will leave it to your honesty and good judgment as to how you use these human-nature levers or any other technique that exerts influence over your fellow men. Some *take-charge* devices in this book are dynamite.

In all events, make yourself familiar with these basic Teleological Actions I have grouped under HUMAN–NATURE LEVERS. Many of us have "favorite" situations in which we are never effective, and the right human-nature lever at the right time can change the way those situations go.

1. Give orders on the assumption that they will be obeyed.

This need not call in the gruff voice and the military manner. But when you tell someone to do something you are entitled to tell him to do, don't imply he has an alternative. Do not act as though there is any question about your being obeyed.

63

The director of a reform school told me he got the best results with his student body when he borrowed a slogan from baseball umpires: *Call 'em loud and walk away.* "When we'd say to a boy, 'Pick up that candy wrapper and put it in the trash can,' then watch to see if he did it, he would consider it an open question as to whether he did it or not. But when we say *do so-and-so,* and turn and walk away, chances are it gets done."

Few of us are in constant contact with young toughs. But the man who annoyed his secretary by asking her to "get the Jones file if you don't mind" was implying she had an alternative.

Remember the motorist who informed the gas pumper attendant that his windshield *was* going to be wiped, *wasn't* it? Asking for good service and giving definite orders go hand in hand.

Take charge of this particular factor—giving orders on the assumption they will be obeyed—and your word literally is worth more, both to yourself and to the other fellow. Many bumps are smoothed on the road of your life. "Orders" may be nothing more than requests, but as long as they are justified requests, they will be carried out.

Now take a clean sheet of paper, and down the left-hand side list all the people to whom you gave orders, or of whom you made requests, today and yesterday. Tell the story briefly: "I asked Miss Williams to take messages for me while I was in conference," "I told Johnny to do his homework" and so forth.

Down the right-hand side of the sheet, rate yourself on each item. Rate yourself *A* if your order or request was made pleasantly but with no hint that the other person might conceivably not do as you said. Rate yourself *C* if your tone was one of apology or contained any kind of KICK ME. If somewhere in between, give yourself a *B*.

Look over your ratings.

Now think about tomorrow and in your mind's eye see yourself dealing with the same people. Pleasantly, with a *please* and a *thank you* as may be called for, but as one who knows what he wants and has enough self-respect to ask for it properly. When tomorrow comes, ACT that way. *It's the way successful men act.*

Notice that very few people resent being asked to do something they are supposed to do. Also notice how many people wait until they are asked!

2. Assume the other fellow will take some step you want him to take, and breeze him right along to the next step.

I examined a new car in a showroom and told the salesman I would buy the car. He praised my good judgment and began to check off items on a list. Did I want an outside rear-view mirror? I did. "Rear-view mirror," he murmured into his list. "And you want our good model radio to go with a car as fine as that . . . and you want two speakers, front and back, for real good sound. . . ?"

I almost bit. I didn't want a radio; I wanted a tape player because I like it that way. But when the salesman assumed there was no question about my wanting the radio—only about how many speakers I wanted—he almost pulled me right along with him.

It reminds me of the way a soda-fountain boss got more people to order eggs in their malted milks for an extra ten cents per malted. When you ordered a malted at that fountain, the attendant never asked: "Do you want an egg in it?" Instead, he'd hold up two eggs and say expectantly: "One egg or two?"

It's really a kind of reverse-twist to the idea of giving another person a standard to live up to. When you catch him off guard, he may conceive he is not doing enough toward his own self-interest and jump right up to the standard *you* prefer. But you may, in fact, be providing him with a status improvement he will be grateful for.

When I was selling those ranch homes in Florida, I found it very easy to run through a check list of expensive landscaping items and merely assume out loud that people would want them. But I added this safeguard for my customers: I always handed them the checked list and told them to inspect it overnight and give it back to me the next day with their written okay for the work to be done. Generally a few items came off the list, but what I lost in immediate profit I gained in reputation for honest dealing.

The fact is that people *will* follow a leader. People *will* let an expert tell them what to do. *The man who knows the answers has a big take-charge advantage.* He is always potentially capable of swinging the action the way he wants it to go before any alternative answers drift in.

A board of directors okayed the idea of looking for an industrial site in a distant state, but nobody ever got orders to do the looking. So somebody's alert assistant went ahead and made contacts with industrial commissions in various parts of that state, estimated costs and labor supply, and so forth. When he then circulated his information among the board members, they made some motions toward getting other opinions, but they soon found the assistant had done all the winnowing; it had to be his choice. The assistant also got the job of vice-president in charge of plant, which he had coveted.

Maybe he then asked the chairman of the board whether he'd prefer one chimney on the new plant, or two!

3. When the other fellow acts in a way that hinders you, tell him he acts in a way that helps you, and watch the results.

Our office boy, Willie, was bright enough, but we wasted endless time undoing his mistakes. He simply did not listen to instructions.

So the office manager told him: "Willie, I've always appreciated the careful way you listen to instructions. I like to work with a man who finds out how to do a job before he tries to do it."

Willie immediately began listening to instructions.

This technique is not used often enough. People shy away from using it because they feel they are insulting the other person. But, in fact, it is surprising how easily people persuade themselves that their vices are virtues—and are ready to accept any compliment as truth. *Hardly anyone knows it when you take charge of his mind.* The reason is simple and important: Very few people know how they appear to others! For example, see how many items you can add to the following double list:

The other fellow says he is	*But everyone knows he is*
an independent thinker (that's what Willie called himself)	too impatient to listen to instructions
sensible about money	stingy
the kind who ties up loose ends	an unbearable fuss-pot
being himself	unheeding of others' rights
not a bookworm	not willing to inform himself
philosophic about his failures	a victim of his Will to Lose

I am sure you were able to add a few items drawn from your experiences with people among whom you live and work. When

Robert Burns wished that God would the giftie gie us to see ourselves as others see us, he was reflecting the gap that exists between one's self-image and the image others have of one.

If you still hesitate to treat anyone the way we treated Willie, remember this *and observe it in action:* When you tell another person he is better than he is, he will accept your opinion as an insight into his true nature. Amazing? Yes. True? *Yes.* Try it and see.

What we did for Willie we did for Willie's good as well as for our own. But the same technique can be used quite wickedly.

A friend once told me he had lost several hundred dollars in a gambling casino, and found he was left with enough to pay his hotel bill with only five dollars to spare. He stashed away the amount of the hotel bill in an inside pocket and decided to bet the five dollars on roulette. If he lost, he'd get out while the getting was good.

So my middle-aged friend walked up to the roulette table. The attractive girl croupier sized him up, gave him a big blonde smile and took charge of his mind. She shouted: "Now here's that big bettor! One side, everybody!"

Everybody turned to see the big bettor. My friend's self-interest changed from *Be sure I can pay my hotel bill* into *You bet I'm a big bettor and I'll show 'em!* (not unmixed with fear of the embarrassment he'd suffer if he chickened out). He dove into his inside pocket, added the five dollars to his hotel-bill money, bet it all—and lost it all.

You've probably heard it said that self-preservation overrides all other emotions. Not so! Hit the right note of emotional self-interest and you can get a man to throw away his life as well as his money. How many men have died in order to keep a flag waving?

So you *can* reach into the other fellow's mind, and as though turning a switch you can tell him what you want him to be and make him live up to it. Fortunately, *most* people have *some* common sense and this technique is not 100 per cent effective. It is surprisingly effective for all that, and I wish you would make the following compact with yourself:

If ever I take charge of another person's mind for my own benefit, I will be sure it is for his benefit as well.

4. Take charge of arguments by maintaining a position of strength.

67

Benjamin Franklin swayed many minds in his day, and he was never a noisy table-thumper. But he kept himself in a position of strength. In his autobiography, he put it in a deceptively mild way.

> I made it a rule to forbear all direct contradictions to the sentiments of others. . . . When another asserted something that I thought an error, I denied myself the pleasure of contradicting him abruptly . . . and in answering, I began by observing that in certain cases or circumstances his opinion would be right, but in the present case there appeared or seemed to be some difference. I soon found . . . the modest way I proposed my opinions procured them a readier reception. . . .

People who don't do it Ben Franklin's way—who vehemently *argue*—may believe they are controlling others, but they are themselves more likely to be controlled. Argument is psychologically (and teleologically) unsound because it stirs up hostility. The argued-at-till-he's-exhausted other party may give grudging consent; but let an old saying state the case: "A man convinced against his will is of the same opinion still."

Let's see how to do it better. We'll merely paraphrase Franklin:

a. Listen to what the other fellow has to say.

b. Tell him that what he says has value and cogency. *But*.

c. Without ever saying he is wrong, show that in the present circumstances some other criterion should be applied, or some other side of the question should be made foremost.

When you tell the other fellow he is right you give him credit. He is then the more willing to listen to what you have to say, and what you have to say will have been in no way limited. Naturally, *your* viewpoint should have something to be said in its favor. But when you keep yourself in a position of strength, your chances of putting your ideas across are greatly increased.

Here are some teleological approaches of especial value in putting across your ideas:

Don't try to prevail against a person who dares not agree with you.

We sometimes meet situations in which a person *must* take a stand, however unfortunate the stand may be. At that time or perhaps all the time he is a man who already has a strong emotional commitment to his position, and you cannot prevail against that commitment. Let him be. If you can't win, stay in a position of strength by at least not being defeated.

Don't follow red herrings when they are drawn across your path.

Stick to your point! You can Ben-Franklin the other fellow by *acknowledging* every point he makes, but don't follow him down every inviting alley.

Reminds me of the judge who listened patiently to a lawyer's many reasons why his criminal client should be let off easy. Then the judge said: "Yes, Counselor, I agree your client never shot anybody. I agree he does not take dope. I agree he loves animals. I agree he never fails to visit his aged mother. But this *is* the third time he has been arrested for armed robbery, isn't it?"

Red-herring types love to take hold of some side issue that has nothing to do with your main issue, and make much of it. That's how it went with a man who complained that YOUR SUIT DRY-CLEANED IN 24 HOURS more often meant 48 or 72 hours. The wily proprietor of the cleaning establishment told him that a day didn't begin at the moment he slapped his suit onto the counter. This led into an argument as to what a day really is, and whether it begins at sunrise, or at sunset, or at midnight . . . and suddenly it was closing time and the customer did not have his suit or any notion of when he would get it.

When you have won your point, try to let the other fellow keep his honor.

This technique is subtle, and is more important than many people realize. It often makes the difference between winning an argument and losing a friend, or making your point and keeping your friend.

A person who gives in to your ideas, under circumstances requiring his open acknowledgment that he does so, is somewhat bruised. Particularly if you have come forward with some unassailable figures or facts that show his figures or facts to be all wet. He ends up with a soul-bruise, and it hurts.

69

So, first of all, the instant you win your victory, *change the subject.* Nothing you can say about the argued topic, right then, will be accepted as neutral comment. Anything you say becomes rubbing it in. So join the other fellow in a kind of unspoken agreement that the subject is exhausted. Don't crow. Don't ever say: "I knew you'd see it the right way," or anything of the sort. Let him keep his honor.

Better yet, if possible, accept part of what he says. Thus, a member of a school board prepared an elaborate plan for a new playground. He then urged it upon the board but saw it defeated for a very valid reason. But when the playground was built, his boss saw to it that a form of primary-grade seesaw he had recommended was installed in it, and he felt much better about the whole thing.

When the other fellow gives himself no escape hatch, be sure you open one for him.

When someone gets angrier and angrier because you won't see things his way, his very anger commits him to his own point of view almost as strongly as the fanatic who dares not have his opinion questioned.

But you stay calm, which means you stay strong. And you treat the other fellow as though *he* were calm. You gain strength because you *do not acknowledge his anger.* Then, if and when he finally sees he has been wrong, he also is free to tell himself that his anger did not get across—you did not seem to notice it—so he can pretend he wasn't really angry. That is his escape hatch. It's the old Chinese system of giving the other fellow a chance to save face.

Now and then you meet the *ultimatum.* You are the credit manager, and you want to give an extension to an account who is having trouble. The president gets his dander up and says: "You give that no-good so-and-so an extension and I'll fire you." Just as you do not acknowledge anger, so do you *never acknowledge an ultimatum.* You Ben-Franklin the boss by saying: "You don't want me to give Jones an extension." Period. Then, as may be indicated, you tell the president that you have investigated Jones's story about slow deliveries and the story is true. And maybe you give Jones the extension and maybe you don't—but if you do, the president can forget he said he'll fire you. It didn't get across. You gave him an escape hatch and everybody is better off. Later on he may refer to you as the best credit man he ever hired.

As a matter of principle, *never acknowledge a threat*. That way, you take a lot of take-charge away from the other fellow.

Don't let yourself be heckled.

Any heckler can keep you from speaking with effect. Recognize his power by throwing it into his face. Say that since what you have to say is worthy of at least three minutes of uninterrupted attention, perhaps you had better take it up another time. The heckler won't like you for saying that, but he shows himself up and you gain allies elsewhere.

On occasion you can insist on communicating *in writing* and getting your answer in writing. Much depends on the occasion, but do this when you can and you make the heckler impotent to heckle. An employer I know could never work peaceably with a certain union representative till he did this.

All you ever need is the slight edge of influence.

To take charge of other people's minds you need not be a Svengali. Most people are not very effective, and when you *are* effective, even a small edge of influence adds up to a great deal. Taking charge need not be done in a spectacular way; but small, repeated take-charge incidents not only build your influence and control over other people's minds, but they also build your priceless *reputation* for having a "magic" control over others.

There is no way to calculate how much such a reputation is worth, but Andrew Carnegie paid Charles M. Schwab bonuses of up to one million dollars a year because he could get the people at Carnegie Steel to do what he wanted them to do.

Henry Ford referred to this ability as being worth more than any other. He was noted for the way in which he surrounded himself with men who extended his own talents, and he said he would *pay more* for the ability to control others than for any other ability he could "buy."

Remember, the magic wand in controlling other people's minds is: *Appeal to their emotional self-interest.*

71

Appeal to their *self-interest,* and traffic your self-interest appeal through their *emotions*. Appeal to their *emotional self-interest*.

Later on I will show you other strong, sure ways to take charge of other people's minds, gain the benefits and build benefit upon benefit. But before you read any further, *go into action.* USE every goal-seeking teleological action I have shown you. Learn how to control and influence others by *doing* just that.

The more you use Teleological Action in your business life, personal life, family life, all of your life, the more you TAKE CHARGE OF YOUR LIFE and make it better and better.

Where we have been:

To take charge of another person's mind, work through his emotional self-interest. Let logic be secondary. Test yourself on a number of emotional self-interest appeals and feel their essential grip and their action-getting power. Notice how successful advertisements appeal to self-interest through the emotions.

Use the great power of asking favors, with its mighty status factor. Smooth away difficulties by giving orders or making requests on the assumption they will be obeyed. You can take charge of another person's decisions by assuming he will take some step you want him to take. People will follow a leader.

Tell a person he acts in the way you want him to act—and get him to act that way. Check your knowledge of human nature by setting down a number of instances in which people show how little they know about themselves. In arguments, hold to a position of strength and follow Ben Franklin's advice: never tell the other fellow he is wrong.

Don't try to prevail against a fanatic. Stick to your point and you'll get your point across. When you have won your point, keep a friend by letting the other fellow save his honor. Maintain your strong position by never acknowledging a threat; instead, give the other fellow an escape hatch so the threat goes unnoticed. Don't let yourself be heckled.

The ability to control and influence others has no top price on it. It is almost a "magic wand" of success. All you need is a slight edge of influence and you are far ahead.

Where we are going:

Coming down to the nuts and bolts of earning money, we next consider your job, what it means to you, and how to answer certain basic questions that guide you toward high-paid job success.

5 Command Your Own Career—I

Finding the Right Job

As a basic action in taking charge of your life, make sure you are in the right job. Definite signals will tell you. The right job arouses and focuses your Will to Win—brings out latent talent and ability that can make your fortune. Should you work for yourself or for someone else? Simple procedures give you the answer, while other simple procedures show you where your future lies and get you ready to go.

"Do you like your work?" I asked the mail-order merchandiser. He was the somewhat "lost" man I mentioned when we were discussing the amazing power of a point-of-view letter—the mournful fellow who had let himself be conned away from his own best line of work before a point-of-view letter got him back on his own main track.

Now here was the same man five years later. He sat in a swivel chair in a big office with high, old-fashioned windows, and the sun streaming through those windows showed all the dust that was afloat. Big as the office was, he hardly had room for his desk, his chair and a table. Piles of cartons—the overflow from the stockroom—filled three-quarters of the space. As we spoke, brisk young men dashed in and out to make up orders, finding a pair of binoculars here, a magazine rack there, a cuckoo clock, a lawn mower sharpener . . . all part of the great variety of goods that a mail-order house can sell.

Down the street, my friend was building a three-times-larger headquarters with air conditioning, a conveyor system and hydraulic

74

loading docks. Meanwhile, he sat amid those toppling towers of cartons, swiveling from his desk to his table while he juggled pages for his Christmas catalogue. He grinned at me a couple of times, fiinally swiveled my way with a huge grin under a mask of dust.

"What work are you talking about?" he asked. "This is *fun.*"

I remembered the disgruntled, beaten-down man I used to know. Now here he was, making five times what he used to make, sparkling with enthusiasm, using twice as much energy as he'd ever thought he could muster, working all day at high speed and calling it *fun.*

Had he found the fountain of youth?

Had he discovered some magic pep pill?

Had he met some great guru of the mysterious East who had wired him in to a mighty cosmic source of power?

None of these. He had found his Will to Win. And he had found the perfect focus for anybody's Will to Win. That is, he had put himself into *his* right job. He had found the most personally rewarding way to spend one of the three vital areas of life.

Work, Recreation, Sleep—Interdependent Areas of Living.

Your day divides itself roughly into three periods. There is a period of work; a period devoted to recreation, eating and so forth; and a period of sleep. Somehow, some people have the idea that you really *live* only two parts of a day; that you work merely for the sake of your recreation after your working hours.

If that is the way it seems to you, rear back and have another look. You are cheating yourself. Work, recreation and sleep *all* are parts of full, enjoyable living. All are interdependent. If you take the point of view that your work is just something you do in order to finance something else you call "your life," you are— morally speaking—throwing a third of your life into the garbage can. Worse yet, that attitude practically assures that you won't earn a quarter of the income you could earn. It is an attitude that makes you full of *won't try* and *don't care,* and everybody gets the message.

Now, not every man who likes his work will show his liking as strongly as does my friend the mail-order man. The drama that attended him was part of his personality, but the world has room for all kinds of people! Whatever may be your basic personality, however, if you think your work is something merely to be *endured* . . . then you are not taking charge of your work, you are losing vast percentages of your possible income, and the take-charge power you apply to your life has gaps in it a mile wide. You had better take charge of your *attitude,* launder it, wring it out and hang it in the bright sunshine for a thorough purification.

And then do some looking and asking and thinking directed toward getting yourself into *your right job.* The right job is a tonic for the body and a fresh bright breeze for the spirit. It is not only part of living, but a vital part of your enjoyment of living. On top of which I have seen the right job open up many a man's earning power to horizons he never before dreamed he could reach.

How do you know when you're in the right job?

If you asked the mail-order man how one knows he is in the right job, he would say, "You feel it!" And he'd be right, in a broad sort of way. We must particularize this *feeling,* however, and connect it with certain patterns of *action* and *thought* that become easy to see and immensely profitable once you and your right job get together.

The following check list offers you a Teleological—goal-seeking—Action which begins when you make your checks as you read down the list. Don't make any check mark unless you're entitled to make it. When you make a check mark, make it good, big and positive. Your goal is to find the phenomena that go with being in the right job.

TA: CHECK ANY ITEMS THAT APPLY TO YOU IN YOUR JOB.

( ) *You feel "at home" in your job.*
Every man who is in the right job agrees on this! One said: "I put on my job like a well-fitting suit." By the same token, when you are in the *right* job you are rid of an uneasy, damaging feeling that so often dogs you when you are in the *wrong* job—the feeling that you are a stranger, a person out of place, a "duck out of water" as the saying goes. The right job FITS you . . . deep down where you live!

76

( ) *You feel all-alive in your job.*
Nobody is absolutely fatigue-proof, but even when you are pretty well pooped after a long, demanding day on the *right* job, you can still find a feeling of happy zest somewhere underneath, just waiting for you to have a breathing spell so that once again it can take over. Most men know how deeply one's *energy* is connected with one's *emotions,* and that deep-down feeling of *rightness* is one of the world's greatest pepper-uppers.

( ) *You are eager to know all about your job.*
Men who are in the wrong job, who take any-old-job for the sake of any-old-income, often seem to be working inside a box. The box contains the man, his job and just enough information and skill to enable him to do the job. A man in the *right* job is surrounded, not by walls, but by horizons. With a sense of joyful discovery he learns *all* about his job and all the extra knowledge about his job and the way it jibes with jobs around it and above it. A man in the right job quickly makes himself a man who knows the answers.

( ) *You have a sense of dedication to your job.*
Since your job is so much a part of you, your dedication to your job is essentially a part of your dedication to yourself. But "dedication" can be misunderstood. It does not mean you do your job to the exclusion of all else in life; that's a defeatist way to live. It does mean that when you work, you live your job to the hilt. You don't hold back any part of yourself from the *job* part of your daily living.

( ) *You make few mistakes in your job.*
Anyone goofs now and then; but you definitely do not *fumble* your way through your work. Also, the mistakes you make tend to be the kind of mistakes that "go with the job."

For example, the manager of a large department store told me that he *wants* his department heads to make at least one big mistake a year in the area of buying. He said: "If a man has not bought at least one 'dog' item that the customers won't touch, I feel he has been too cautious."

A man in the right job—at home in his job, knowing the ins and outs of his job, tuned in to his job—must still take chances because so much of business consists of taking chances. But a man in the right job tends to take the *right kind* of chances. (A man, like a turtle, begins to make progress when he sticks his neck out.)

(   ) *Your job arouses and focuses your Will to Win.*
Many a man I have counseled has told me in his own words that when he was in the wrong job or jobs he found it hard to see the SUCCESS factors in himself. But when he found that grand and glorious right job, he saw himself instantly as a SUCCESS and all his SUCCESS factors came roaring through.

This is not quite the end of the check list. The final item is an all-inclusive one. Do not seize upon it as a means of bypassing the six particularized items you just read. In fact, go back and count the check marks you made. If you made at least three, you may be in the right job. You may just need some time for learning. You may need some time to let your self-confidence take hold after years of its being kicked around.

If you have done justice to the first six items that help you know if you are in the right job, then consider, with care, the seventh, a big, wrap-up item:

(   ) *As you do your job, you act, think and feel like a "pro."*
A pro takes a professional attitude toward everything he does. From his first day on the job, he is not an amateur. He finds out the answers. He knows what he is doing; he needs no prolonged learning period to take away anything tentative or fumbling in his approach.

A pro develops a kind of sixth sense that helps him anticipate trouble and often stop it before it starts. I see a pro when I see a man who works, not merely at his *job*, but at his *business;* that is, a pro salesman does not merely sell his product, but also knows why and how and where it is made and everything else about the *business* behind it. And I see a pro when I see a man who is easy, confident and *pleased*

78

every day at his job, who rolls with the rebuffs and laughs them off, who sees new opportunities and is always ready to handle them because he has such a condition of *oneness* with his job.

A pro puts himself into *his* right job, and a pro and his job are the best of friends; a pro and his job always help and strengthen and profit each other. *Does that fit you?*

Your point-of-view letter can be a great help in steering you toward the work that is right for you because you see your life's PATTERNS OF SUCCESS—a matter we are going to come back to very shortly.

Should you run your own company—or should you work for someone else?

Leonard K. was on the wrong side of the fence (for him) and was forty-five before he knew it. Starting as office boy, he had become foreman of a small plant that made floor-maintenance equipment—waxers, polishers, sanders and the like. He was well paid, earned good bonuses, and he had also made a little from inventions which improved the company's products.

Leonard liked to relieve his tensions, which were numerous and hurtful, by puttering in a home workshop. Out of this puttering one day came a model of an entirely new home-maintenance product. (Since it is not yet on the market, I cannot tell you what it is.) Leonard packed up the model and took it to work to show to his boss. But instead he took it home without having unwrapped it. Suddenly, as though his entire world had changed, *he wanted to manufacture and market the item by himself*.

With the feeling came a sudden surge of energy—and more. He realized he had been taking life just as something that *happened* every day. Now, he told me, he felt as though he had at last gotten his hands on his life's steering wheel.

He told his boss he was leaving. The boss pointed to the security he was giving up, offered him a double bonus, did everything possible to keep Leonard from quitting. The boss even got after Leonard's wife to "talk some sense into him." But that's where he met a surprise. The wife said something wonderful had happened to

Len, and she wouldn't do a thing that might spoil it. And it *was* wonderful . . . his new zip and zest, his joy at having found himself, his eager anticipation of his great adventure.

Finally, after some months of getting ready, he is in it all the way. His production line is ready to roll. He is going to distribute through a chain of supermarkets. When your wife comes homes with a gadget about the size of a small book that runs on its own renewable-forever battery that you recharge overnight . . . a gadget that helps make housekeeping quite a bit easier . . . it will be thanks to Leonard K.

Meanwhile, Len has borrowed money in order to get started, and in other ways has had to stick his neck out. But he is his own boss. And he is one of those men who should be his own boss. That is what makes it *good,* and his *right* job.

Now here is an important point: Everyone knows that the man who runs his own show usually stands a better chance of making big money than the man who is on salary. True, nowadays in large companies you can find numerous men whose salaries are right "up there," and they also have stock options, pension rights, profit-sharing funds and other arrangements that can amount to very handsome money. Still, the man who owns his business is the man who is more likely to make the bonanza.

It is that reason, the profit angle, rather than aptitude or liking, that puts many men into businesses of their own. Which is why the business world is full of misfits who would be happier, healthier and often richer in someone else's business. They just don't take care of a business the right way; they don't get the hang of it no matter how many years they try.

Do it right or don't do it at all.

Take the matter of capitalization: Most businesses that fail, fail in their first year, and they fail because they don't have enough capital to keep them going until they are "over the hump." This is well known. Yet people go on starting businesses without anywhere near enough capital. They seem bent on showing how misplaced they are. Subconsciously, they often expect to fail (remember the Will to Lose?).

Perhaps worse than failing is *almost* failing. This can go on for fifty years. If you want to see exactly what I mean, prospect about among the small retail stores of any city. A good percentage of them belong to men who have no talent for business, no *feel* for business, no business being in business for themselves and probably no good reason for being in business at all.

You can often judge the near failures by their flyblown, messy display windows. Even a shoemaker can make his window look as though he's in business for keeps! And a dry cleaner and tailor can arrange things so that his sign, CUSTOM SERVICE, does not look like an outright lie. Most retail stores are run by men who never learned how to act interested in a customer, nor how to buy their stock wisely, nor how to get over the inertia that keeps them from moving to a better location, nor how to write an ad, nor how to approach the man at the bank with any more than a hangdog expression that practically begs the man to say no.

But before *you* go into business, do some soul-searching. *Do you have what it takes?*

TA: BEFORE YOU EVER GO INTO BUSINESS FOR YOURSELF, CONSIDER ALL THESE ITEMS.

Do you have patience enough to wait until you have money enough, or have made arrangements to be factored?

Do you have the stamina to accept the hazards of business that affect even the smartest businessman?

Are you willing to work hard for long hours, perhaps doing a dozen different jobs, until your business gets rolling?

Have you a "head" for the thousand-and-one details of a business; the payroll complexities, the tax headaches, the need to deal with many people and know the answers for everyone, the problems of finding and keeping the right employees . . . and whatnot?

Yes?
No?

While you search your soul, turn back to the chapter on setting up your lifetime goals. One of the suggested goal files was devoted to considerations of the small business. Read it over again.

If you have a business "in the family"—if that would be your only reason for getting into business on your own—think long and hard before you do. Many a man who takes over his father's or his uncle's "concern" finds he has trapped himself into a well-paid, ulcer-ridden misery.

Sometimes a man who isn't quite sure which side of the fence is his side does well as a salesman. There you run your own business, in a way, but you attend only to selling. *Few people make more money than a good salesman.* Selling, in fact, is marvelous training, and often worth a try to see how it suits.

"To thine own self be true!"

And if the deepest part of your truest self will accept nothing less than your being the boss of your own business—go to it, my friend! And go all the way. The ancient adage *Anything worth doing is worth doing right* is, or should be, a business cornerstone. Do it *right,* and the boundless force of your own enthusiasm will make everything fall into line.

Testing your aptitude.

You can get good help in knowing yourself and knowing the kind of work that is best for you. Here is an area in which too many men refuse to spend a little money that can come back to them several-thousandfold. When you pause to consider how much it can be worth to you to put yourself into the right job . . . surely it is worth something to find out what that job should be.

For some men there never is any doubt. But if you have doubt in your mind, don't be ashamed of it. There are many, many kinds of jobs and some men must search longer than others to find the right one.

All of us, however, have definite areas of talent that point us toward the right job and all that it means in terms of money and life-success. Do you know you own best talents? For a preliminary view, go back to the point-of-view letter or letters you wrote. You listed a number of successful actions. See if they show *patterns of talent.* Often they do.

Take that as a beginning. Now consider: Many universities and other institutions, and many private firms, work with psychologists and educators and counselors to create full-fledged *aptitude tests* to show any man his best talents, his inward drives and other success-factors. Is it worth, say, from twenty-five to one hundred dollars of your money to take some of these tests? It can be the most worthwhile investment you ever made!

What aptitude tests can tell you about yourself.

Aptitude tests are generally written, but may also include interviews. You should take three tests, each from an entirely separate organization. Not one. Not two. *Three*—because the tests vary. When three aptitude tests agree, say on half a dozen cogent facts about yourself, you can depend on it—that is YOU. And it's like a dark shade being lifted from your life because now you will look back and see abundant proof that that *is* YOU. Aptitude tests can tell you, for example:

> If you are the kind of person who is at his best when he works on a team or when he works independently
> Whether you have realistic social evaluations: a true view of the world insofar as the interaction of people is concerned
> What your favorite after-work activities show about yourself
> Your ability to relate one idea to another and see patterns of logic
> Your ability to present ideas clearly
> Whether you are visual-minded
> What childhood influences may still be hindering you
> What the real trouble was in some job that bothered you
> Your general level of self-confidence
> Whether you like to make other people think the way you do (important for a salesman)
> Whether you are good at showing others how to do things (important for a foreman)
> Your level of patience
> Your tendency to lead or your tendency to follow

Your arithmetical talent

Your verbal ability, spoken and written

Your formal education as compared with the require-
ments of various jobs

Your self-education as compared with the require-
ments of various jobs

What your failures show about you

What your successes show about you

Whether you are fitted for a particular job or type of
job (which generally is a separate test in itself and
may be given to you by a prospective employer)

And that is only the beginning!

If you can sit down with a psychologist after he has studied your
"battery" of tests, you will be in for a very illuminating experience.
As one man put it, after I had insisted he spend seventy-five dollars
on what he had called "rigmarole": "It wasn't rigmarole, but something highly perfected and, let me tell you, pretty darn impressive.
That man who had met me for the first time sat there and told
me all about myself. Things I knew, mostly, but wasn't looking
them in the face. I came out of that office with the name of my
right job as clear to me as though I had it engraved on stone."

For guidance in finding aptitude tests and having them adminis-
tered to you, check with your local library. Another good source is
your board of education. A good many universities have counseling centers open to the public; just check your classified telephone
directory for these and for private testing firms. Or, inquire at the
personnel department of any large company and the chances are
you will receive sympathetic help.

Assuming you are not one of those men who knows clear as
daylight the kind of work he wants to do . . .

Assuming you have had several jobs and by now you know
what it is to feel something always lacking in a job . . . and/or
lacking in your response to that job . . .

Assuming you have noted, from time to time, what a man can
do when he is in the right job for him . . . how a man's *right* work
fulfills him and strengthens him and makes his every work-thought
and work-action worth more and more . . .

Don't you think it's time to present yourself with some aptitude testing?

If you still hesitate, then take it on the strength of my own broad research into jobs and men, and on the strength of all the experienced businessmen and counselors and psychologists who helped me write this book. And proceed *now* with this Teleological Action:

TA: TAKE THREE GOOD APTITUDE TESTS AND THEN ACT ON THEIR GUIDANCE TOWARD YOUR RIGHT JOB.

This chapter has presented you with a weighty challenge. And, concerning jobs, there is a lot more to come in the next chapter— most particularly, about the precise Teleological Actions that build you and your income rapidly upward in any type of job.

So we'll end this chapter with a story—a story in which I am the nonhero—and the way I got something of a come-uppance may be the part you enjoy most.

The store that was "no good."

It was 1947, I had recently surrendered my wartime commission, and I was nosing around in real estate, which definitely is *my* preferred line of work. Early in the year, I got in with a company that ran a chain of hardware and home furnishings outlets. By September I was pretty well running the company, and making more than three times my starting pay. I had the knack and the knowledge it takes to find good stores; my judgment was paying off, and I felt pretty good about it. In fact, I felt rather egoistic. In fact, I was getting swell-headed.

One day I drove a couple of hundred miles to look at a store in a town where we had not yet done business. I arrived hot and sticky, the town was hot, and I was an hour early. I phoned the real estate company that handled the store, but they couldn't send anyone out to show it to me at that moment. They asked me to wait and assured me that their Mr. Harris would be there right on time.

Mr. Harris was indeed right on time, and found me in front of the store, rather disgruntled. I had decided it was too small, and I didn't care for the location. Also I didn't care much for Mr. Harris. He must have been twenty years my junior. Judging by the condition of his face, he had only recently begun shaving.

He was nervous, too. But I noticed he walked up with the store's key ready in his hand and said nothing, save to introduce himself, till the door was opened and he had ushered me in. It would have been almost impossible to refuse to step in.

"You're a stranger in town, Mr. Summerhill," he said as he switched on the lights, "so I brought along a city map . . ." And he was unrolling it and taping it up on a wall in a jiffy.

"How did you know I was a stranger?"

"I took the liberty of inquiring about you at the Chamber of Commerce. They knew your name" (I noticed the logical but definite flattery) "but they said you've been in business downstate. Ah, here we are." He'd already circled our location in red on the map. "Now you see, here's the bus terminal pretty close by. And here's the railroad station . . . "

"That's all very well," I said brusquely, for it was high time *I* took charge of the situation. "This is a business neighborhood, however, and I wish someone in your organization had made that clear. We want our stores in residential neighborhoods."

"I know you can back that up with a lot of experience, Mr. Summerhill," young Mr. Harris said a bit nervously. Still, he knew better than to contradict me! He went on, pointing to the map with a slightly shaking hand, "Here's a really special situation, though, Mr. Summerhill. See, right nearby here is the factory district. And then right here we have a big concentration of downtown offices. Now, what does that add up to? Plenty of people coming in from the suburbs or other parts of town, going to work, and going home again. By bus and train, which takes them right past this—"

Now he's in trouble! I said to myself. Aloud, I cut in, "No they don't. They get into their own cars and drive straight home."

"Oh yes! A certain percentage of them! Our survey showed that 12 per cent of the working people in this area do drive to and from work. But it's not likely ever to be much more than that because this city is not going to break up its downtown with a lot of parking spaces and garages and freeways and such. We're doing it the other way. We keep our bus lines and commuter trains running good service by giving them a tax break. So they are going strong and most of the workers are glad to save the expense of a car, or an extra car. We even have certain times when lanes are kept clear for fast bus traffic." He saw he had me listening. "So you have a lot of people going to and from the depots, morning and evening, and you can see this store is right where the foot traffic goes. Isn't it, Mr. Summerhill?" He showed me on the map.

I heard myself saying, "Yes."

"And it seems to me they'd find it mighty handy to have a store right here where they could pick up tools, paints, all kinds of gadgets, maybe snow shovels in season. Men like to buy hardware items—but I guess I don't have to tell *you*."

"Uh—quite right. However! This store is too small."

"It *is* smaller than some others, Mr. Summerhill. But let me show you how much basement storage room you have" (he had the trap door open) "and it's a nice, dry, well-lighted basement, with room for a conveyor right along *here*. And look at this catalogue, Mr. Summerhill. Oh, I'm sure you've seen it, with your interest in stores" (I hadn't, but I kept quiet) "but will you have another look at this pegboard arrangement for showing a lot of items in a small space? Sort of encourages people to help themselves to small items while salesmen assist them with more expensive items. I understand it's the big thing in merchandising . . ."

It is now, but it was new then. I asked him for a tape measure. He had one. I did some measuring and some thinking. I didn't say much. Finally I said I was going to make a personal survey of the foot-traffic flow past that store. Mr. Harris offered me a little click-counter.

The upshot of it was, we took the store I had been so sure was not suitable. It worked out well. We called it The Big Little Store That Has Everything.

Mr. Harris (not his real name) told me later that he had had just five days of real estate selling experience when he sold me that store.

I told him he had instinctively known how to show me *I could have what I wanted,* even though I had about made up my mind that I couldn't. *That* is great salesmanship.

He had made himself ready to deal with me, ready to turn my negatives into positives. He had given me expert testimony: the town map, the survey, the town's very philosophy of keeping its business center alive while other business centers were falling to pieces. He had let me know that I, too, was a well-informed person.

Above all, he had taken charge of the situation; he had taken charge of *me*. I could see "pro" sticking out all over him.

He looked pleased but puzzled. "Well honestly, Mr. Summerhill, the way I did it . . . isn't that the way it just has to be done?"

He is a big man in real estate now, with a full hundred people working for him. I look back on that day with interest and with humility. And I give you the story as a perfect example of the right man in the right job.

Where we have been:
When a man is in the right job, he can get so happy and interested that his work is like play. Even a "quiet type" finds a deep happiness in doing the work that is best for him, and any type of man soon finds that his own right job can zoom his income.

Work is part of life, recreation is part of life, sleep is part of life. When you are in the right job, you never think of your work as being merely a preparation for "living." You fit your job as though it were a well-tailored suit. You find deep reserves of energy. You are eager to know all about your job, see all its horizons. You have a sense of dedication, hold nothing back. In the right job you make few mistakes. Over-all, you act, think and feel like a "pro" when you and the right job get together.

Should you run your own company or work for someone else? The decision is basic and important. If you run your own company, be sure you start with enough capital. Accept the hazards of business. Be willing to work hard for long hours, for a while at least. Make sure you have a "head" for business details.

A business in the family may be good for you or it may turn out to be a trap. You may find your best job is in selling, where a great deal of money can be earned. Or you may begin as a salesman and later go into another phase of the same business.

How do you know what kind of work is best for you? If there is any doubt in your mind, take three good aptitude tests and note

88

the pattern they show. The money you spend for such guidance will come back a thousandfold.

Where we are going:
Continuing with considerations of your work and pay, we now set up a great guiding rule you can apply to any work situation. If you never knew the real difference between a man who has built-in job success and a man who never attains it, you will see it now.

6 Command Your Own Career—II

Working with a Will to Win

Your basic thinking about your job can either make you ill-paid all your life or zoom your income into the six-figure bracket. One simple motto, presented in this chapter, assures that your pay is always catching up to you. Coupled with certain actions, this motto makes sure you never get stuck in an interim job. The motto, the actions and your treasury of take-charge qualities team up in a comprehensive drive toward big money.

Ask yourself this important question: What do you mean when you say, "I have a job"?

For the majority of men, *I have a job* means: *I have a place to go five days a week where I perform certain motions, and I am paid to do this.*

For a certain significant minority, however, it means: *I have a place to go five days a week where I accomplish certain services at which I enjoy using my skills, and for which I receive high rewards.*

For those of you who are of that positive-minded, healthier and happier minority, this chapter presents Teleological Actions that make any man worth more and give him a 99 per cent dependable assurance that he is going to earn more, and again more, and again. This applies anywhere on the ladder between office boy and president . . . at any stage of a man's working career.

And yet these Actions, important as they are, are not so important as the principle that backs them up. Before examining the

Actions themselves, we are going to examine that principle. You will see how solidly and surely it takes hold of any job situation and how firmly it builds a career of any kind. It is the *one* all-embracing principle that governs success for a man in a job.

Let me give you two stories that show the principle at work. The first story is about a beginner in business who began *right;* the second is about a man past sixty who could have stayed in the stymied and frustrated position in which circumstance tried to push him, if he had not so well understood that a man's inner resources *never* fail.

1. *"My boss was worried because he couldn't find me a better job in the company fast enough."*

So said the younger man. He began as a house-mail boy—a collector and distributor of papers—in a huge insurance firm. His job was to push a little cart around acres of floor space . . . first picking up from one OUT box and another OUT box and another OUT box . . . then putting down in one IN box and another IN box and another IN box.

According to the standards proclaimed by his colleagues in the distribution center, this man had a good, secure spot. All he had to do was build up seniority. He was sure of a little raise now and then, and he had a solid road to a pension. They assured him that nobody ever got fired in that company if he just kept his nose clean.

What they were illustrating all too well was an old story: It is *your* choice as to whether you soar on your Will to Win or sag on your Will to Lose . . . whether you take charge of your life and boost it into the sunshine, or stay wherever careless happenstance may steer you, even if it is in some dark and forgotten corner.

My friend belonged to the happy minority who don't like to live in dark corners.

As he went his rounds with his cart, he studied the flow of paper traffic. In a little while he found ways to do his job more efficiently. (Others in the distribution center laughed at him and asked him what he was going to do with the time he saved.)

He now studied the layout of the various forms he picked up. He found ways in which some of the forms could be condensed and improved. (Others in the distribution center told him he was bucking for corporal.)

The young man won a fifty-dollar award for a suggestion he put into the company's suggestion box about forms. He now paid attention to all the numberless details of operations and equipment with which a big company can save or lose a dime at a time, thousands of times over. He also took a course, two evenings a week, on office management methods. He won another award for a suggestion on a better arrangement of certain desks and files.

One day he walked into personnel and suggested he ought to be made an assistant office manager. He told what he knew. The interviewer raised his eyebrows and sent him in to see the boss. That was when the boss worried about not finding him a better job fast enough, lest he move onward and upward in another company.

Leaving out discussion of interim steps . . . this same man is now readying himself for the job of General Manager in charge of home office operations. The salary is proportionate to the job, and stock option privileges and other benefits run up his reward quite a bit higher.

And oh, yes . . . he'll still get a pension!

2. *"Therefore be it resolved . . . "*

Robert S., an aging bookkeeper, always had yearned to be a certified public accountant. Kept from this ambition by a series of personal and family misfortunes, he nevertheless made a special study of his company's accounting methods, financing, factoring arrangements, tax position. His financial analyses became greatly respected. When any question about the company's money came up, the officers always made it a point to "ask Bob."

Bob got some good raises, but a man's real progress is made in quantum jumps. Where could Bob go? He was already sixty-two.

One day the board of directors passed two resolutions. With one, they extended the sixty-year age limit that had applied to new corporate officers. With the other, they rescinded a requirement that the company's treasurer had to be a certified public accountant.

Then the chairman of the board asked Bob to drop in—to find out he was now treasurer, and that his salary had been raised from twelve thousand a year to thirty thousand.

92

What principles did you observe in those stories?

Read them again. What do you see?

A *Will to Win*? Right!

The *confident expectation of success*? Right!

The power of being *the man who knows the answers*?
Right!

Making a particular use of *one's goal-winning power*?
Right!

Taking charge of the opportunities all around you?
Right!

*"The world makes way for a man who knows where
he is going"*? Right!

You can see quite a bit more. But here is where we look for and
see one great all-inclusive *principle,* the golden framework that
holds every other principle you apply to getting ahead on your job,
the principle to apply before you go on into *method,* the principle
that backs up every job-advancement method, the master take-
charge principle that applies to every man who wants high income
and high satisfaction out of his job.

Here it is. It takes only twelve words to say it.

KEEP THE LEVEL OF YOUR WORK ABOVE THE LEVEL
OF YOUR PAY.

Read that out loud.

Remember it, know it, feel it, *live* it.

Now pause right here.

TA: PRINT THE FOLLOWING WORDS ON A FILE CARD:

I AM GOING TO KEEP THE LEVEL OF MY WORK
ABOVE THE LEVEL OF MY PAY.

Keep that card with you. Invest a quarter to get it laminated so
that it does not become dog-eared. Keep that card in your pocket.
It becomes the solid framework of your soaring job success.

When you empty your pockets every evening—and I hope you
have that habit, common with well-organized men—you are going

to see the card. Don't stop with merely seeing it: READ IT OUT LOUD.

Then stop and think, then and there: *What did I do today toward keeping the level of my work above the level of my pay?*

Put the card right on top of your wallet or your key case. That way, you'll see it again in the morning. READ IT OUT LOUD again in the bright light of morning. Stop and think right then, right there: *What am I going to do today toward keeping the level of my work above the level of my pay?*

This reading aloud is an action of the simplest kind, pointing the way toward other actions.

Its power to make you *think* is tremendous.

Its power to make you *feel*—feel yourself growing more and more accustomed to keeping the level of your work above the level of your pay; feel yourself accepting yourself and liking yourself because you keep the level of your work above the level of your pay; *feel* like a man who gets ahead and so *thinks* and *acts* and *is* that kind of man and *proceeds* that way—this power is so terrific, you simply have to live the experience. Then you know.

Keeping the level of your work above the level of your pay does not happen of itself. But the action of constantly reminding yourself that *this* is your approach to your job will lead you constantly, confidently, into other action that lifts the level of your work—and pay—and *joie de vivre*.

Now try an experiment.

TA: TELL SOME ROUTINE WORKER, SOMEONE WHO'LL BE SATISFIED ALL HIS LIFE WITH VERY SMALL PORTIONS, THAT YOU KEEP THE LEVEL OF YOUR WORK ABOVE THE LEVEL OF YOUR PAY. WATCH HIS REACTION.

You did something like this before when you told a person of no ambition that you intended to fill a particular high-level job. As before, you will find yourself on the receiving end of raucous laughter, or at least of a pitying smile.

And then, it is almost certain, your low-income friend will ask you why in the world you want to cheat yourself. In one way or

94

another, you will be told that if you keep the level of your work above the level of your pay, you are cheating yourself.

Know that this is a conditioned answer; that the folkways of the Will to Lose group demand this type of answer. Anyone who gives little in return for little is touchy about being "caught dead" doing anything extra for his boss. If you think differently, you have to be wrong. Notice how defensive and irritated a low-level worker can become on this point.

Don't argue. Stay on your own level. You see matters differently. Rejoice!

You can see that, far from being cheated, it is quite the other way around.

When you keep the level of your work above the level of your pay, you automatically make sure that any job short of your goal-job is an interim job. You will not ever "get stuck in a job."

When you keep the level of your work above the level of your pay, you simply make sure that your pay, your position and your job satisfaction are always catching up on *you*. And this is very different from constantly and anxiously *pursuing*. Besides securing the hundred thousand a year I consider a reasonable goal for any man who takes charge of his life, an avoidance of tense, anxious pursuit is far more likely to give you that goal without your also achieving ulcers.

When you keep the level of your work above the level of your pay, you keep yourself *in a position of strength*. And if you have not been in the habit of keeping yourself in a position of strength, you don't know what you've been missing.

Now then:

The methods that keep the level of your work above the level of your pay.

One might logically present several dozen methods. I give you just a key few, each completely tested and broadly inclusive. As you read each one, stop awhile and think. See how it may apply to *you*. These methods become wondrously effective as soon as they are personalized and pinpointed. A pin penetrates because its force is applied to a very small area—right where you want to see results.

95

TA: KNOW YOUR PRESENT JOB; DO YOUR PRESENT JOB.

A man with a college degree complained that another man who had only a high-school diploma had been promoted right over his head. Moreover, the complainer's degree was no mere A.B., but a degree in business administration that should have been exceedingly useful.

The trouble this fellow had was a popular trouble. Once he got his job, all he did was to rest on his degree and go through the job's necessary motions.

The man who could not loll on a sheepskin also went through his job's necessary motions. The big difference was that he performed every motion with the extra push that marks a willing worker. As with the college man, the high-school man considered he was doing an interim job. But, in his case, interim job or no, the job was well learned and well done.

In speaking of goals we spoke of the fact that the attainment of interim goals must precede a major, this-is-it attainment. Interim goals, however, require their own taking charge, their *complete* attainment. Let it be part of your bedrock probity that you do any job that is yours as well as you possibly can, simply because it *is* your job during that year or that week or that moment.

Also, the good worker flies a highly visible signal flag. I know how many times I have watched for, waited for, practically prayed for signs that men on my staff were worthy of promotion. In preparing to write this book, I found out that executives everywhere perform the same kind of watching and waiting. The mournful fact is that the majority of men in jobs, even in jobs several long steps above the bottom, are content to go through the motions and wait for a "tenure" raise. The man who does better than that practically flies a flag for his boss to see. I have even found myself in the interesting position of scurrying around to find a better job for a man who certainly should have it—before he goes somewhere else.

"Lower level" is a relative term, but broadly speaking, it is in the lower-level jobs that we form the habits of attention, conscientiousness and comprehensiveness that mark the man who rises. It is on his lower-level jobs, done right, that a man forms the priceless habit of doing everything right. Bear in mind, too, that lower-level jobs—even more than higher-level jobs—give you opportunities to show your Will to Win. All the way up, you proceed by victory upon victory. *A man at the top is a man who has made himself used to winning.*

TA: IDENTIFY ANY SPECIAL OPPORTUNITY YOUR PRESENT JOB MAY OFFER.

You saw how the house-mail boy did this, and moved onward and upward into a different type of work. The bookkeeper, on the other hand, extended his present job onto a higher level of the same type of work. Both approaches have success-power.

TA: WHEN YOU SEE THE OPPPORTUNITY YOU WANT TO EXPLOIT, DO JUSTICE TO IT. LEARN WHAT YOU OUGHT TO KNOW.

The young man with the mail cart did this; so did the older man in the other prototype story.

Getting down to nitty-gritty, you can see that doing justice to an opportunity often mean *learning something.*

Keeping the level of your work above the level of your pay often involves *learning something.*

Winning a promotion often involves *learning something.* Sometimes you can learn on the job. But sometimes a man depends on learning as he goes when he ought in addition to present himself with more definite, more formal learning.

"I haven't the time," you say. If that thought popped into your mind . . . *nuts!* I don't think "I haven't the time" is true with more than one man in ten thousand.

Today's economy gives you the time! I began on a six-day week, eight hours a day for real. My father worked nine hours a day. His father worked twelve hours. As the work week grows shorter it hands you self-improvement time on a silver platter, it strews rose petals in your path. An evening or two a week can be filled with interest and profit . . . for the man who can break away from the boob tube.

Your own company may be willing and happy to send you to

school. Your local library can surely steer you to all kinds of business-oriented courses.

Should you be unable to identify any particular subject you ought to know about—always a temporary condition—give thought to the general business skills. Any man in any business is the more ready for any advancement when he is knowledgeable about such matters as:

Typewriting (to make you independent of your secretary now and then)

Simple accounting

Mechanics of merchandising

General aspects of finance

Principles of advertising

Most of us can profit by a course in memory training. Or in speed arithmetic. Or in speed reading. I can tell you by virtue of experience that skills of this nature are founded on utterly simple gimmicks. Find out the gimmicks, practice, and you are that much more efficient, that much more *wide awake* inside your several billion brain cells.

Most especially do I recommend speed reading. Paperwork is all around us; printed information floods us; knowledge *is* power. You may not believe this until you try it, but the fast reader generally remembers more of what he reads than does the word-by-word man.

TA: SEE YOUR COMPLETE PICTURE.

See the forest as well as the trees. Learn about the business of which your job is a part. And learn about the industry or service of which your company's business is a part.

Get started on this broadening process and you'll find it fascinating. Find out:

> How your company is organized; its various divisions or subdivisions; its foreign offices, if any.

> Your company's markets; distribution setups; general approach to selling, retail and/or wholesale. Who buys your company's product?

The product or products, service or services you help to create, even if they are in branches of the company far removed from yours.

The competition; how their products or services may differ; how they go to market.

Read those many-ways-useful trade magazines. Read the statistics and discussions put out by the U. S. Department of Commerce or local or regional business organizations.

When you do this, you are performing in a way that is automatic with upper-echelon men. The broader your view, the more you tend to belong where you look out through an upper-echelon window.

You also give yourself on-the-spot aid in making more money because you can see opportunities in an entire trade; you may even learn you are in the right trade but the wrong company.

You also show up well in an interview. The president of a fifty-million-dollar corporation told me: "We like to find men who can carry on a lunchtime conversation about industry trends, or government regulations, or the like. Not that this is a substitute for knowing one's particular job, but it does show the kind of awareness that is part of any good executive."

TA: MAKE YOURSELF A MAN WHO KNOWS THE ANSWERS.

This has come up before, and naturally enough, since it overlaps so many other take-charge qualities.

With our friend the mature bookkeeper, it was a fairly obvious process to nail down the kind of answers he should know. For a less experienced man it may not be so obvious.

A story goes: A man put on a remarkable show with trained birds. He got those birds to do all kinds of tricks. When asked how he did it, he replied, "I think the way the bird thinks."

A good salesman thinks the way the customer thinks.

And a man who wants to qualify for a better-paid position ought to think the way the person now in that position thinks.

Observe the problems faced in that higher-up position. Observe the situations that come up. Out of this you can form questions, and for a handy aid in forming logical questions, use the words Who, What, Where, How, When, and Why. *What* does the advertising manager want to know about our new product? *When* must the chief engineer have his budget ready? *Why* is the sales manager making a concentrated selling effort in the Southwest? And so forth, on whatever may be the appropriate level of approach.

You may find it surprising, and certainly it is rewarding and mind-broadening to put yourself in the shoes of someone in a higher-up job, or even in a merely different job. It is possible to synthesize experience; make your mind a laboratory; feed in data; *insist on an answer.* You can make yourself *feel* and *think* like a man in a different job. You can know so much about the job before you get it that you are ready for an upward move in a surprisingly short time.

TA: KEEP YOUR OWN KIND OF COMPANY.

Above and beneath and all through this matter of success runs the *mystique* of success. Keeping your own kind of company—that is, positive-minded, optimistic, successful people—can be said to have its completely practical side. I cannot but agree that it is good to have the right people know you. But . . .

Beyond this there is something that doesn't get pinned down so easily.

A salesman spent a certain assigned hour each day at his headquarters. At this hour he found the place full of bellyachers. They ran down the sales manager, sneered at their customers, talked endlessly of how life had cheated them and kept up a flow of general complaints.

(Notice as you go along that unsuccessful people tend to be perpetual complainers. When a successful man finds fault, it's a fault that *counts.*)

Well, here was a man set among a lot of bellyachers in their second-day shirts, and the bellyaching got under his skin. When he'd go out to sell he'd have a feeling of gloom, which is not the feeling out of which sales are made.

At last he asked for and got a different office hour, knowing it was an hour when he would fall in with enthusiastic, self-confident, successful men. His sales rose 30 per cent.

The majority of those who fail set themselves up for failure; you know that. Now bear in mind that if you consistently keep company with downgraders and gloom-mongers—easy to find among failures—*some of their Will to Lose is likely to rub off on you.*

Fortunately, it works the other way too. An atmosphere of success brings out your own success attunement.

When a group of successful men get together at a meeting or at lunch, they seem to say: *I am competent, you are competent, we all are competent men who enjoy being competent.*

Each of us is an individual; yet each inevitably is part of a crowd. It is almost impossible not to absorb *something* from the company you keep. If an adverse influence is long continued, something will get through.

I do not suggest that you absolutely refuse to associate with anyone who is dominated by his Will to Lose. Now and again I have seen a man—generally a young man—attempt to insulate himself against all but success-oriented thinking. Such prigs rarely win success. They simply are insufficiently human. A well-rounded mind needs to be fed with a wide variety of impressions. So don't get the idea you are going to "catch something" if you merely chat with a failure.

Just be sure that insofar as you can manage, your *norm* is the company of successful men. Then you participate in the very spirit and dynamic of success.

And, by the way, you can find successful people, imbued with the Will to Win, at any level of income. You simply won't find them at the same income level very long.

This chapter does not stand alone.

These career-advancing Teleological Actions may have seemed rather short and simple. Remember, however, that they represent inclusive methods . . . categories rather than particularizations of action. Find where they fit you. Apply your own pinpointed action.

You will find that because these Teleological Actions have such a wide wingspread, they also have a terrific upward thrust.

And they do not stand alone.

Back in Chapter I you took charge of your WILL TO WIN, the great central dynamo that whirls the wheels of victory. You discovered your own four-square foundation of success-factors you have used again and again.

In Chapter II you took charge of your SELF–RESPECT. You saw how to build your self-respect in small affairs and in large until your entire range of actions shows your belief in yourself as a person who expects the best and gets it.

Chapter III focused your self-respect and your Will to Win into a great GOAL–WINNING POWER. Now you can *see* your goal, see the way to attain your goal, fulfill yourself with everything that means *wealth* to you.

In Chapter IV you saw how much of a man's success depends on his honest and constructive ability to take charge of OTHER PEOPLE'S MINDS. You learned simple techniques that sway others to your way of thinking, and saw how a small advantage here and there can give you a many-times-multiplied advantage in life.

Chapter V showed you the tremendous importance of putting yourself in the right job, whether you work for someone else or go into business on your own. It showed you that a man's work is most likely to make his fortune when his work is truly part of his life, truly personal.

The present chapter has carried on the theme, concentrating on the man in a job who wants the high salary and high income-augmenting benefits that come to the executive today. Above all, this chapter has given you twelve significant words, KEEP THE LEVEL OF YOUR WORK ABOVE THE LEVEL OF YOUR PAY, a motto and talisman of high potential.

Time and time again in pursuing the comforts and joys of life-success—whether within a company or as the head of your own company or as a salesman or in any of the professions—you are going to display your Will to Win, show the strength of your self-respect, take charge of other people's minds, win your goals because you know *your* goals.

And so you are possessed not only of the definite types of action that lift a man upward, but also of the inward qualities that must stand behind those actions. No action toward wealth and happiness exists of itself; it is an index of an entire personality.

Where we have been:
To some men—men who work all their lives for small pay—a job means merely going somewhere and performing certain motions. To the man who really succeeds, a job is the source of satisfaction and of constantly increasing reward.

Over and over, the motto that lifts a man ahead of others is: KEEP THE LEVEL OF YOUR WORK ABOVE THE LEVEL OF YOUR PAY. Seen through the Will to Lose, this looks like a way to cheat yourself. Seen through the Will to Win, it shines forth as a power-packed way to make sure your remuneration always has to catch up to you, which means you almost automatically move higher and again higher.

Print on a card: I AM GOING TO KEEP THE LEVEL OF MY WORK ABOVE THE LEVEL OF MY PAY. Read this aloud three times a day. Back it up with areas of salary-raising action:

Identify any special opportunities your present job may offer.

When you see the opportunity you want to exploit, do justice to it. Learn what you ought to know.

See your complete picture.

Make yourself a man who knows the answers.

Keep your own kind of company.

Remember that this chapter does not stand alone. Everything that has gone before in TAKE CHARGE OF YOUR LIFE helps to give your career vigor and meaning.

Where we are going:
In the next chapter we pause to consider the priceless part of your wealth—your health. At the same time, you will realize that the same factors which make you healthy can be of great aid in making you wealthy.

7 Build Your Most Basic Aid to Health

Ready and waiting for thousands of years, a handful of words gives an all-inclusive health secret. Building on these words, you can take charge of the actual, personal influences that affect your health. Also, you will see exactly how people worry themselves sick, get heckled into sickness, and in other ways allow their minds to damage their bodies. Perhaps recognizing yourself, you proceed toward setting up a great natural defense against illness which, of course, is also a great natural aid to a happy and successful life.

My good friend, my family physician, says he is sorry he told me the following story. He says it can be construed as an anti-doctor story. What do *you* think?

One of Dr. X's patients was a very tense little man who suffered from a variety of nasty skin disorders. Tension is often associated with skin disorders, so Dr. X decided he'd first calm down this nervous fellow, then give him some medicine for his skin.

The twitchy little man accepted the tranquilizing pills and went home. A few days later he came back with a clear skin, and announced he felt better all around and all of his dreadful itching was gone.

The physician himself was impressed. "So all you needed was to calm down! The tranquilizer itself was the cure! Tell me, how many of the pills did you take?"

The patient hesitated, grinned and said, "Doctor, *I* never took those pills. I put them in with my wife's vitamin pills, and *she* took them."

Now, a psychosomaticist, the latest type of specialist, might have found out first of all that the itchy patient had a wife who nagged and heckled him. The wife gave the man a continual emotional hammering that showed itself, as such hammerings often do, in an unfortunate physical way. When the wife got calmed down with the tranquilizer, she stopped nagging; the husband was able to relax, and so no longer had any emotional reason for maintaining his rashes and itches.

One hardly knows whether to laugh or cry on hearing such a story.

I don't think it is at all an antidoctor story. Let nothing I say in this book make you feel that I am in any way antidoctor. In fact I have a healthy respect for the progress of medical science.

By and large, however, we make or break our own lives. And so, in this chapter, I dwell upon our tremendous and terrible talent for *making ourselves sick;* and correspondingly, every person's ability to help his own health *from within.* Which does not throw all medicine out the window, but does insist that the first and foremost guardian of your own health is *you.*

And here is a motto, a talisman, a bedrock guide to help you keep healthy. It comes from the King James Bible, Proverbs 17:22: *A merry heart doeth good like a medicine; a broken spirit drieth the bones.*

In more modern language, we say: *Your emotions can make you sick; your emotions can make you well.* And again: *Your health depends a good deal upon the way you get along with yourself.*

Any way you want to say it, remember it! And once you are aware of the merry heart versus the broken spirit, you see them at work all around you, upgrading health or downgrading it sometimes to the point of death.

The connection between a band of gold and a cold.

Some years ago I saw a fine musical show called "Guys and Dolls." At one point, a doll named Adelaide came downstage and sang mournfully about her troubles. She wanted a husband; and also she was bothered by colds. And she saw the connection. She warbled that a woman who waits and waits for that little band of *gold* can develop a *cold.* And you can give her a *shot* for whatever she's *got* . . . but that's not what she needs, and so forth. The way the audience laughed showed how many people were saying to themselves: *So true, so true!*

While a scraping from Adelaide's throat might have revealed the presence of streptococci, another person with the same streptococci might feel fine. Adelaide's reason for being so susceptible to colds was (as it very well could be in real life) her unmarried state. She wanted a man. Without a man, she was subjected to a long-continued frustration, which is exactly the kind of thing that "gets us down." We generally rise to meet an emergency—a package of trouble that begins, rises to a climax, and ends. It's the long-term emotional hammerings, or even tappings, that appear to cause a glandular imbalance and open the door to ill-health.

To another girl, being unmarried might be the merest trifle, surely nothing to get bothered about. And just so is one man made literally sick by an overdemanding boss, while the fellow at the next desk says, "I can't see why you let old Fuss-pot annoy you."

At any rate, if you take a shot for what *you've* got, and the relief is only temporary, maybe what you've got more basically is a set of dismal emotions.

———

Your "broken spirit" can make you very sick.

Psychosomatic conditions (Adelaide and the itchy man had psychosomatic conditions) can run all the way from colds to high blood pressure to strange cripplings to, possibly, diabetes; to built-in fatigue, maybe to asthma, to ulcers, to all kinds of digestive troubles, to heart ailments . . . nobody knows where the list ends.

The word *psychosomatic* itself tells the story. It refers to a condition visited by the mind (*psyche*) upon the body (*soma*). A few generations ago, it was generally estimated in professional circles that one-third to one-half of all illness originates in the mind. Estimates today run as high as 90 per cent. Dr. Flanders Dunbar remarked that it really is a question of *how much* emotional influence exists in *any* illness. With hysterics, there is a fantastic grip of mind upon body. When the grip is broken you can have an instantaneous faith cure that logic is helpless to explain.

Then too, the *body* can bully the *mind*. Henry James remarked that we don't necessarily run away because we are afraid; we may

106

be afraid because we run away. As a human being you are one dynamic entity. You act, feel, think, act, feel, think, act, feel, think, act. . . .

And *re*act physically, too.

In the last chapter I mentioned that ulcers can arise from a long-continued process of frantic *pursuing*. You can also get rich that way. But any man who is wealthy and *healthy* is far more likely to evince the "merry heart" of the Will to Win . . . the all-embracing *confident expectation* we are going to talk about soon.

The present chapter goes hand in hand with the one to follow. Here, as a major Teleological Action, we'll set up the goal of discovering what kind of emotional factor may be heckling *you* into illness. I used to go at this in a very dead-pan way, but experience has shown me that a bit of drama helps. So then:

TA: SET UP A ROGUE'S GALLERY OF YOUR AILMENTS AND CHOOSE A LIKELY PSYCHOSOMATIC SUSPECT.

Sit down now with a pad and pencil. List any characteristic illnesses that plague you and/or any physical discomforts short of illness that follow you around—like constantly getting up in the morning with a headache.

If you find you get unholy joy out of making that list, you are probably a hypochondriac! Take it easy. You are probably not so sick that six or eight entries won't cover. The human mind/body is so complex, it's quite unusual for any adult to go through a day without feeling a twinge or a creak somewhere.

All right; you have now listed no more than six or eight forms of personal physical distress. One or some of these may be psychosomatic in origin; that is, *guilty*. So, like a detective, you inspect those six or eight shifty-eyed suspects. And you play a trick known to all detectives. Instead of accusing each suspect of being guilty, you accuse each suspect in turn of trying to take the rap. That is, examine each on the assumption it is *not* psychosomatic.

Discomfort in the midriff may then be traced to your habit of eating meals that are too lengthy and weighty.

Headache may stem from that third drink last night.

Backache may be due to a sagging bed.

Muscular pain may arise from trying to keep up with your teen-age son in singles tennis.

In short, cross-examine every ailment or discomfort and you may dig up some very logical, unpsychosomatic basis for its being.

When you find such ailments, send them away with a warning. Those that still remain in the lineup may really be psychosomatic.

Check over what is left of your list. While practically any physical manifestation may originate in the mind, the following, when persistent, are among the most likely candidates:

Skin conditions
Recurrent headache, especially migraine
Respiratory-system troubles
Generally sore and or constricted throat
Indigestion
Constipation
Diarrhea
Nausea
"General weakness" and/or continued fatigue
Continued stiffness or near crippling of one particular
    limb
Pain in the back of the neck
Lump in the throat
"Gall bladder" pain
Gas

Now, when you find a likely suspect, you may feel an emotional resistance to the idea that it is psychosomatic. This masquerades as a "logical" resistance; you "find out" convincing reasons why your emotions can have nothing to do with it. Suspect it all the more!

Not everyone can search himself in depth. Sometimes it takes a psychiatrist to do it, or at least a good lay counselor. But I want you to try. I'm a pragmatic so-and-so, and I tell you that when a man really tries to see within himself, he often can. I'll follow up in a moment with various clues to help you.

When you find a likely indictment write the name of the probably-psychosomatic ailment on a 3 x 5 card. Use a separate card for each such ailment. Then:

TA: LOOK FOR AN ACCOMPLICE—A MOTIVATING PERSON OR CIRCUMSTANCE—OR A REASON WHY YOU GAIN BY HAVING THAT AILMENT.

The motivating person for the itchy little man's itches was his wife. The motivating circumstances for Adelaide's respiratory troubles was her spinsterhood.

But what is all this about *gaining* by having an ailment? Yes! It begins with the little boy who feels "just awful, Ma" when it is time to go to school, but makes a swift recovery when it is time to play baseball. And it goes on and on, up to the point at which it seems some people die just to "get even" with someone else . . . and I assure you, this phenomenon is to be taken seriously.

Well now, you get off into a quiet place, perhaps someplace where you can walk up and down as an aid to thinking. You have pinned down an ailment that may very well be psychosomatic, rooted in your emotions. *What* circumstance or person can you now associate with the occurrence of the ailment? Why, Who, When, Where, How?

Someone you live with? Someone you work with? A circumstance that occurs every day? Periodically? A load of guilt for some misdeed that is with you almost all the time? Some guilt fastened on you in childhood? A wish to keep yourself from doing something that might hurt or disgrace you? Loser's limp of some variety? Boss? Wife? Partner? Parent?

Now read the following examples and make a large check mark next to any that may apply to you. Use judgment and imagination. The specific factors in any one of these stories can be switched around ad infinitum, so that *boss* in a story may be *wife* in your own experience; or your ailment may be quite different from the one mentioned. Look for a *basic circumstance* that rings a bell in your mind, and make that big check mark. Also note how strong is the factor of *gaining something* by being sick.

A man had indigestion every night after supper, but

109

he never had indigestion after breakfast or lunch. Investigation showed that supper was the one meal he ate in company with his wife.

No matter what a college student did over the weekend, he always had a terrible headache every Monday morning. Monday morning was the time for the regular weekly quiz in his worst subject.

A man suffered from disabling symptoms of bursitis in his right arm. For years he had wanted to punch someone, but knew that it would result in his getting beaten up.

The X ray showed nothing wrong with a woman's spine. Nevertheless she had terrible spinal pains when she went to bed. (Except when her husband was away on a business trip.)

A minister never was hoarse except when he preached on his favorite topic, *guilt*. He had a lurid past he had to hide from his congregation.

A rich man had ulcers. He was filled with hatred of people and fear of losing his money.

Three times in five years, a man who ran a family business came down with a heart attack (or at least the symptoms thereof). In each case, the attack came when his son announced he wanted to leave the business.

The son stayed on in the business because he couldn't very well leave when Pop was so ill. But the son had a lot of diarrhea.

A man came from an asthmatic family, suffered from asthma all his life and was especially distressed by roses. When a psychotherapist shoved a bouquet of fresh roses into his face, the man almost expired on the spot—until he was shown that the roses were artificial and had no odor whatsoever.

A man of thirty-five became sexually impotent for no reason his physician could find. He had, however, been

110

pushed into a job he wasn't ready for, nothing was going right and he lived in constant fear of being fired . . . *failing*.

An unloved wife developed various symptoms for which the indicated treatment was hot baths at a distant and expensive spa. This forced her husband to spend money on her.

An unmarried woman of forty insisted on taking "healthful" walks in tight shoes that made mincemeat of her feet. She became quite insulted when her physician remarked that self-torture can be a substitute for sex.

Poor Momma! In song and in story and in reality she sets herself up as the professional sufferer, the self-sacrificer, the collector of injustices. She never is free of some pain she is sure is "serious"—but never mind, it is her duty to nurse *you*. You come to realize you are expected to feel guilty because you can't help her. Later you may come to realize that is the way she wants you to feel.

The poet Elizabeth Barrett, while she lived in her father's home, was an invalid. Thus her father could not inflict upon her the various cruelties he inflicted upon his other children. Also, in her way, she was able to torture her father. When Robert Browning took her away and married her, she was an invalid no longer.

A man had money enough to keep his wife in the suburbs and a succession of mistresses in town. After he had first won then gotten rid of a dozen intimate female friends, he had well established that every one of them gave him headaches and dizzy spells. A wise counselor suggested he give himself the medicine of a good conscience. He became faithful to his wife and his ill-health went away. Even a frightening heart murmur vanished.

A businessman found himself hardly able to get out of

bed, he felt so weak and sick. This went on until he sent the tax collector what he really owed.

A man went from surgeon to surgeon trying to find one who would agree with his own diagnosis—that he should have his gall bladder removed. At last he found a surgeon who did remove the gall bladder. Once he had convalesced, the same pain returned. So he decided it must have been something else (maybe his appendix; it didn't really matter) and went shopping for another surgeon.

Did you meet yourself in any of those dark alleys? Some of the stories require a bit of explaining. The son of the boss, with his diarrhea, showed his emotional *rejection* of his father's business. Rejection of some drastic kind is also illustrated by the man who went around having operations.

The asthmatic who came from an asthmatic family illustrated an "inherited weakness" which was really a conditioned expectation; everyone *expected* him to be asthmatic, he was treated that way, so he took it up in early childhood as his accepted way of life. This happens over and over. There does appear to be physical inheritance of a "weak spot" in some cases. You need not ever have the kidney trouble your father and grandfather had, for example; but if you go through some physical or emotional strain that really hurts you, it is in your kidneys that trouble may show up. Don't lean on this, however!

The man who went impotent because of fear about his job was one of millions who in some way *act out* their emotions. Fear of one kind of failure became real failure in another direction.

The man who had all the girl friends, and some other figures in our stories, showed the beating that one's conscience can give the body. Physical manifestations caused by an affronted conscience often serve as a punishment we believe we deserve. Here too you gain something by being sick!

Your conscience and your sense of guilt.

Conscience, as Shakespeare said, "makes cowards . . ." and also heroes; frightened people, inhibited people, physically crippled people, all kinds of people. Conscience feeds on our sense of guilt. And the sense of guilt is not something you are born with; guilt is something every child *learns*.

Yet the guilt complex is an inescapably human trait, part of the complexity of mind that makes us human. It is hard to say how we could have a civilization without a number of inhibitions enforced upon the individual—wherefore a guilt complex, so that you generally enforce those inhibitions upon yourself. And of course there are the many overlapping inhibitions that extend to business, to family living, to marriage and every other activity that brings people together.

So it is not the guilt complex as such that we are fighting. It is only the excessive (and generally localized) guilt *pattern* we want to bring under control, so that you don't go through life beating down your health and shortening your life because of your own depressed emotional reactions.

Bear in mind, above all, that there are no absolutes in this matter of guilt complex. Some men suffer when they are unfaithful; some men thrive on it. Some men suffer when they cheat on taxes; others boast about it. But then, as we know well, a circumstance that defeats one man will strengthen and inspire another—and that is only another side of the same coin which is labeled YOUR LIFE IS WHAT YOU MAKE IT. Generally speaking, a man who keeps his actions within his own society's definition of "allowable" is going to be happier than a man who does not. There is a vast range of wealth-creating, health-extending, enjoyable action possible within that framework.

TA: COMPLETE YOUR CARD OR CARDS AND KEEP ON REVIEWING WHAT YOU HAVE FOUND OUT ABOUT YOURSELF.

By now you'll have anywhere from one to half a dozen cards filled out. Add to each what you may have discovered, if anything, about the "accomplice" in your emotionally caused ailment; the person or situation responsible for what ails you. And also anything you can figure out as to what you may gain by being ill or crippled.

Each card, then, contains discoveries; and each offers food for a great deal of thought. Keep on shuffling those cards, reviewing them. But do not proceed in a state of anxiety. Overanxiety (a form of fear) is all too typical of those who suffer from emotionally induced illness. And don't worry about any card that has very little on it.

The secret is not to be *wrested* from your cards. The chances are very good that it will come to you—in due time. As you repeatedly refresh your conscious mind with the results of your detective work, the items find the deep places of your mind where they can, as it were, exchange notes with each other. You will stir up long-ago memories; you will become aware of certain patterns that run through your life; you will see when and why and how you react differently to different people.

Most men who have tried this method found that one or two of the cards seem to feed back their information most strongly, and call for extra notes. When this kind of "nudging" calls attention to your note on any heavily suspect ailment, and especially if you have had treatment for that ailment, this may be *it*. And the circumstances associated with that ailment also may be *it*.

One man said: "I thought I was feeling nauseous" (a rejection symptom) "because I was driving to work on such a bumpy road. After a while of playing with the cards I made, I realized I was nauseous when I drove *to work*."

The pain of discovery.

To discover the emotional cause that makes you ill can in itself be quite an emotional experience. It is often preceded by a period of resistance because it can be *painful* to find out, and we instinctively shy away from distressing situations. Psychiatrists find many a man who doesn't want to know that his parents filled him with a feeling of unworthiness; at the age of forty or fifty he still finds it painful to admit that his parents could have been wrong.

Watch for the phenomenon of resistance at any stage when you set out to look within yourself. And don't blame yourself for it! It is very human!

When you find your breakthrough at last, painful or not, it is a moment of electric excitement. With years of misery behind you, suddenly you know you have found a way out. This discovery alone

114

can result in a vast improvement of health and a new "merry heart"—a great lift in spirits.

Before, it seemed you were doomed to go on as you were—suffering. Now you see you are only displaying *the result of a conditioning process* . . . of which mighty few are engraved in stone!

You can often change the influence to which you react with illness. Or *you can change your reaction*. Even knowing the nature of your reaction is a beginning in changing it.

One man's meat IS another man's poison.

The great psychiatrist Alfred Adler pointed out that our lives are formed by our *interpretations of reality*. We do not govern ourselves by what really exists. We govern ourselves through our *interpretations* of what really exists.

A spider walks onto a picnic tablecloth. One person reacts to this real situation by screaming and running. Another captures the spider and studies it with great interest.

Two people look at a four-ounce tumbler that contains two ounces of water. The optimist says, "It's half-full." The pessimist says: "It's half-empty."

One of my favorite stories comes out of the experience of that grand old master salesman and philosopher, Napoleon Hill. During the 1920's he made a mint, bought himself a big estate and two Rolls-Royces. He lost the estate in the 1929 crash and found he was glad to get its burden off his back and make a fresh start. Others, who lost considerably less than he did, were pulled out of rivers weeks after they had jumped in.

All these were different interpretations of reality! It comes as a great surprise to many men that they continually *interpret* what comes to them through their five senses. Some find it hard to believe, but I have never met a man who didn't at last believe it after he had thought it over.

You can see that interpretations are personal matters, based on a wide variety of previous conditionings which make us choose to react in one particular manner . . . perhaps to say *meat* when the other fellow says *poison* . . . perhaps to say *poison* when he says *meat*.

But there is nothing *absolute* about a reaction. *You can change*

115

a reaction. Do it by ACTION—the one apex of the ACT–THINK–FEEL triangle that is always under your control. For practice:

TA: DELIBERATELY CHANGE SOME DEFINITE EMOTIONAL REACTION.

Does something in your life consistently make you angry? Try laughing at it! The first laugh comes hard. The tenth laugh feels natural, and your entire attitude changes.

Does something in your life consistently cause you to be afraid? Try to find a ridiculous side to the situation. (By *fear* I do not mean the physical fear that goes with, say, meeting a tiger on a jungle trail. That kind of fear is necessary for self-preservation. I refer to moral fear.) Here's a story:

A department head in a large organization told me that every time he was called to a conference with the company's president, he shook with fright. In fact, he had been told his job was in jeopardy, which helped not at all when he had to face the president, a man of imposing dignity and snarling positiveness (and ulcers). A conference was approaching. What to do?

I took up my pad and drew a picture. I am no artist, but the picture was clear enough. It showed a man sitting behind a desk on which a sign displayed his name—the company president. He wore a suit jacket and a tie, but below the jacket he wore no pants.

"That is the way to see him when you enter his office," I said. "In purple-striped shorts, with his skinny shanks showing. Get a set of crayons and color the boss's underwear purple and green. Color his socks bright red with blue polka dots. Draw holes in his socks. And *see him that way when you enter his office.* If you then spend your energy in suppressing a grin, you will find it impossible to be afraid."

It worked!

Nothing but a change of reaction.

You can change practically any reaction. Here and there throughout this book you have been shown many ways to change reactions—beginning with a great change from "broken spirit" to "merry heart"—the changing implement being a point-of-view letter, which in itself was an exercise in "merry heart" reaction.

It is no news to you that you can change your reactions! If you never before saw this process as an aid to removing an irritant from your life, and therefore a mighty aid to health, see it now! Moreover . . .

You can often improve your health without ever knowing why you were sick.

As a lawyer expressed it: "I may never find out what was making me sick, but I did find out I was capable of living above a lot of irritations and annoyances. If the other fellow could give a cheerful interpretation to things that bothered me, why, so could I. Now I feel better, I get along better with others, everything is better."

I am not forgetting that now and then we simply have to *get rid* of something that is hurting us. Sometimes, after years of doing it symbolically (through nausea, etc.) a man finds the courage to do it for real. It may be a wife, it may be a job, it may be a nagging old mother who has to be sent to live elsewhere. It can require a truly agonizing decision, but it has to be done. I can only suggest that in a very drastic case you should have professional help.

It pays (other people) to worry about your health.

"Daddy, what made you lose all your hair?"
"Worrying."
"Worrying about what, Daddy?"
"Worrying about losing my hair."

Bear in mind that you are constantly subject to influences that make you worry about your health even if you have nothing to worry about. In watching certain TV commercials, it seems evident that the entire population suffers from the jitters, raw nerves, headaches, indigestion and complete inability to sleep.

Don't get all wrapped up in the "latest scientific discoveries" about health. Your doctor, if he is a good doctor, will confirm to you that the vast majority of "great new aids" don't last long, and in ten years' time may give way to quite the opposite "scientific finding."

Whereas a method we might call the-value-of-cheerful-optimism-in-maintaining-health has been consistently accepted, proved and re-proved for thousands of years!

If you think you have something really wrong with you, let your physician find it out. Otherwise, one of the best approaches to thinking about health is to put it out of your mind! Your body always tells *you* when it really is not in working order. Don't *you* try to tell *it*.

Once more—keep the right company.

I have noticed from conversations during lunchtimes and coffee breaks that any office has its corps of hypochondriacs and that they tend to seek each other out. Listen to them for five minutes and you are ready to have dangerous palpitations, or whatever is in style that day. As the next chapter will explain in more detail, we have a vast power to communicate our moods to each other, so, choose the right company! Go around with people who approach life with drive and enthusiasm, with people who are not afraid to enjoy themselves, with men who are successful at their jobs, with people who do not harp upon their health.

Remember how many people *prefer* that you worry about your health, even worry yourself into ill-health. Think of the millions or billions of pills sold each year by advertisers who scare people into believing they need them. I recommend that you *never* swallow a pill without your doctor's say-so.

Even charities scare us. We have been hagridden by the fear of cancer, for example, far beyond the statistical chance of its occurrence. The TV sets of the nation reek with snake-pit programs that make you feel queasy above the neck if the previous program—a magnificent drama of heroic hearts and hysterectomy—has not already made you feel queasy below. Reminds me of a ditty that was going the rounds a few years ago:

> His ailments are endless
> Exotic and rare,
> All promptly developed
> After watching Kildare.

For a windup, I bring you back to: *A merry heart doeth good like a medicine; a broken spirit drieth the bones.*

That is one of the few statements in this world you can accept at face value.

In my mind, it separates itself into an old-fashioned cadence, almost poetic:

> *A merry heart*
> *Doeth good*
> *Like a medicine;*
> *A broken spirit*
> *Drieth the bones.*

Let "merry heart" cover a lot of ground . . . merry laughter on occasion, or a quiet smile, or the inward smile that sings along with your Will to Win, a heart still lifted despite some setback, a mind/body that rejoices in love, the tonic happiness of goals seen approaching and of goals won, the quiet joys of rest well earned, friendship and family life, everything that is warm and wonderful. A merry heart doeth good like some cosmic medicine yet undiscovered. It helps to make you rich—but enough of that! Rather see "merry heart" as a core talent for enjoying every day you live.

Where we have been:
Whether you say it in biblical terms or in modern language, it is true that your emotions can make you sick and your emotions can make you well. It is also true that the body can bully the mind, so that your very actions can bring on a state of mind that is damaging and unhealthful.

Simple "detective work" may show you the source of some emotion that is damaging your health. You list your consistent forms of physical distress and you relate them to your life's circumstances. Also you may recognize yourself in any of the several case histories; but remember, the principals of those case histories may play different roles in your own life.

Be patient in letting your stack of file cards bring out what you want to know. Their secret will come to you as you familiarize yourself with your own notes, and as you repeatedly remind yourself of your own life's circumstances.

119

Few of us realize how strongly our lives are formed by our emotional interpretations of reality. Facing real situations, we handle them through our own viewpoints. But you can deliberately change your emotional reactions. When you attain a generally cheerful and positive attitude toward life, you can often improve your health without ever knowing what it was that made you sick.

Remember, it pays to worry about your health; that is, it pays other people. A cheerful outlook, a *lack* of worry, a "merry heart" is your best defense against illness and your best and most constant source of strength.

Where we are going:
Continuing to consider your emotions, we come to a process that takes patience, but, once mastered, this process makes sure you maintain and increase the gains you have made. You can always be right on the track toward healthful achievement—and the kind of wealth you can spend.

8 Take Dominion Over Your Emotions

We think of ourselves as logical beings, but it is our emotions that often help us or hurt us. Through a simple conditioning process, you can root deeply into your personality the great governing mood, I HAVE A CONFIDENT EXPECTATION OF SUCCESS. The same conditioning process can also give you its equally important companion mood, I AM CONSISTENTLY CHEERFUL AND OPTIMISTIC; MY HEART IS MERRY. Once you take charge of these two moods, they take charge of you. Working together mightily, deep within your essential being, they help to build sure success in your career . . . they help to build and guard your health against any damaging emotional influence . . . they help you to remain healthily successful all the way up the ladder . . . and at the top.

Right now, as wide horizons of fortune-improvement, happiness-improvement, *self*-improvement open before you . . . as you find out more and more about the simple actions that turn the tides in your life . . . *right now* . . .

TA: CHECK THE MOOD YOU ARE IN.

Invest a minute in pinning down your present mood, or general state of emotion; it can be one of the best investments of time you ever made.

Why?

Because the mood in which you approach this book, or the mood in which you approach the entire subject of self-improvement, has

121

a great deal to do with the amount of reward and satisfaction you get out of life.

In fact, I assign as much importance to your *mood* as you read this book as I assign to your actual reading. The wrong mood sets up an inward barrier against absorbing the secrets of success. The right mood brings those secrets shining through.

So, right now, cast upon yourself the inward-searching beam of self-discernment that belongs to every man. Decide on your mood. Find, in the list below, the mood that most nearly corresponds to *your* mood and check it boldly.

> Glowing with the confident expectation of success
> Interested
> More or less interested
> Just reading to see what the book has to say
> Getting to feel that all these success-methods may be too much for me to undertake
> Feeling more and more that these methods just won't work for me
> So anxious about my future that I know I'll go on being helplessly stymied by worry no matter what I read
> So downhearted, discouraged and disgusted that I refuse to believe there is any way to help myself

You probably noticed how the list proceeds from a high level of positiveness at the top to a low level of negativeness at the bottom. The closer to the top you rate yourself, the more you aid your own vast potential for self-improvement to go to work for you, like a friendly giant.

Most men know their moods change, usually many times each day. Few realize the great extent to which your moods are *under your own control* and can be *deliberately changed*.

Just stop to think how a passing mood can affect your interpretation of reality. Think what it could mean to you if you could set up a far greater proportion of optimistic moods, constructive moods, cheerful moods, to help you keep that interpretation swung toward the successful, healthful side.

In particular, we tend to be possessed by some all-embracing mood, or climate of emotion, which in a sense becomes our "char-

122

acter." The Will to Win is such an all-embracing mood. And so is the Will to Lose. Only moods! Nothing to do with logic or "common sense." But your "mere" moods, especially the general moods that you tend to live with, can make you or can break you.

Successful men have a favorite mood.

Keep the company of healthy, successful men and you soon feel the broadcast vibrations of their favorite mood, the emotional climate that forms the foundation of their thinking. It is *the confident expectation of success.*

It is a victory-bringing mood because it sets up *victory* as one's normal condition. *Defeat* is simply out of context. You may now and then acknowledge the reality of a setback, but it has nothing to do with the essential *you.*

It is a healthful mood because it avoids a great deal of inner conflict; it makes every worry a passing worry.

It is an efficient mood. Your confident expectation of success may be likened to an automatic pilot, a goal-seeking device which is installed on many ships and planes. Like this device, your expectation of success senses any deviation from a desired course and takes instant steps to correct that deviation.

It is a mood that makes sure you learn from your mistakes. Having the expectation of success, you truly evaluate your mistakes not as disasters but as experience.

You can see what it means when *confident expectation of success* becomes your governing mood, the pivot of your character. And that is not yet the entire story. This master mood may be likened to a generator which supplies a constant charge day by day—and then, in a time of emergency, you can rely upon it to supply an extra blast of terrific power.

The man who faced the loss of all he owned.

Some chapters ago I mentioned W. Clement Stone, the Chicago insurance executive who turned a hundred-dollar investment into an insurance empire worth well over half a billion dollars.

At one time fairly early in his career, Mr. Stone managed an agency for a parent company whose headquarters were some distance away. The agency prospered. While the parent company had the legal right to terminate the agency agreement, there seemed no reason why they should do so. Planning for expansion, Mr. Stone heavily committed his funds and his credit. And *then* he found his franchise was going to be taken from him!

Stone stood to lose all he owned. Someone's mind had to be changed almost instantly, and the mind was a very tough and stubborn one back in the home office.

Stone, a master salesman with his own full measure of expectation of success, did not immediately reach for the telephone. First he marshaled every reason why the franchise should not be canceled. Then he sat quietly awhile, alone in his office. Completely relaxed, he summoned his reserves—not merely his usual expectation of success, but the great emergency charge that takes hold of every fiber of one's being. When at last he reached for the phone, when at last he made contact with that stubborn mind a thousand miles away, every syllable he spoke and every nuance of expression were keyed to *taking charge* and *winning*.

The stubborn mind at the home office had its own reasons for furthering its own desires. But Stone had gathered an expectation of success that simply could not be put aside by any negative influence. Gradually his confidence enveloped the opposing mind. He spoke for half an hour and he kept the franchise.

It turned out to be a good move for all concerned.

Notice, please, that the confident expectation of success is not a smoke screen behind which lies emptiness. Your confident expectation of success is, rather, a rallying force for all of your experience, knowledge, hard work and self-respect. The automatic pilot will do no good for a ship that sinks in a small storm because it was badly constructed.

But when a man has built into himself what it takes to succeed, then the confident expectation of success becomes the final catalyst that makes everything work together. Without it he still may be "all right," but a man can live fairly well and still miss out on ninetenths of his potential. With it, he gets going and *goes*.

And it is only a mood—automatic with some men, but available to any man who puts an honest basic foundation behind it. It is a mood, a climate of emotion, and you have an enormous amount of *control over your emotions*. YOU CAN TAKE DOMINION OVER YOUR EMOTIONS.

What I am going to show you now is an emotion-controlling method that is close to magic.

TA: HOW TO GIVE YOURSELF THE DEEP, LASTING EXPECTATION OF SUCCESS.

1. *Every day, at the same time, go to a room where you can be alone, quiet and comfortable.* In that room, seat yourself in a comfortable chair; that is, a chair that is comfortable for *you*. Some people relax best in an easy chair; some relax best in a straight chair. Do not lie down, however, or you may go to sleep.

2. *Even as you enter the room, as you dim the light, as you kick off your shoes or do whatever else helps to make you comfortable, let the conditioning process begin to take hold.* Do not act as though you were in any way anxious or hurried. It is important to ensure that there will be no interruption; then you will not act as though you must rush to get everything done before the interruption occurs. Also, you have arranged this time so that it is not time "stolen" from some duty, so you will not act as though you feel guilt.

Even as you enter the room, you embark upon this pleasurable undertaking in a wholehearted, peaceful, assured manner. Do not carry tensions to the chair. I have found it helpful to stand awhile before an open window, swaying gently from side to side, letting the arms hang loosely, blinking slowly. Various planes of vision . . . the window frame . . . something close by, outside . . . something farther away . . . move back and forth in a pattern that requires no meaning. The late, great Aldous Huxley recommended this gentle swaying and blinking and thoughtless seeing as a means of "letting the world go by." Do it a while; and when you are quite ready to sit down, be seated.

3. *Check your position for comfort.* Experiment will find the best position for you, but at first take a position which has proved its worth. Keep your feet flat on the floor; let your hands lie loosely on your thighs, palms down; hold your head in a natural upright position or lean it lightly back against the chair if the chair-back is high enough.

4. *State your mood-objective to yourself.* Or you may wish to

125

have it written in advance on a card you now draw from your pocket and read slowly (however you may write it in your own words): I AM GOING TO ATTAIN A CONFIDENT EXPEC-TATION OF SUCCESS.

As you do this, cast your thoughts ahead briefly to a specific situation in which you expect success. Do not involve your thoughts in the mechanics of the situation. Merely see yourself being success-ful, as in getting a job you desire or persuading someone to change his mind or whatever it may be. See the successful *conclusion*.

State your mood-objective again. I AM GOING TO ATTAIN A CONFIDENT EXPECTATION OF SUCCESS. You have cut down the sensations you generally get from your surroundings. Alone and quiet, comfortable and free of tension, you take several deep, slow, relaxed breaths and feel how good it is just to sit there, alone and comfortable and quiet, alone and quiet . . . alone and quiet. Wait quietly, breathing slowly deep down in the waistline area, letting out each breath slowly and with the utmost ease.

5. *When you are truly quiet and filled with peace, you may find your mind wandering off into reverie-images.* Peacefully and with-out any sense of urgency, recall your thoughts to yourself. The lamas, or monks of Tibet, have a way of keeping thoughts from wandering: They visualize a river, with their thoughts—misty gray shapes—on the other side of the river; then they call their thoughts back across the river and once again the consciousness turns in-ward. It is very difficult to think of *nothing;* but your central thought . . . CONFIDENT EXPECTATION OF SUCCESS . . . can be gently recalled and recalled until it seems to arise from deep within, floating within the mind rather than requiring any concentration.

We are used to effort. This process requires no effort; it requires a state of being we may call no-effort. In belief there is no effort; it is simply *there*.

6. *The first three or four times you attempt complete emotion-control, you may go no farther than the stage described above.* Should you feel your mind restlessly getting back to matters of the day, should this tendency become overwhelming, it is better to stop. But you have not been defeated. You are gathering experience.

One day in your comfortable chair, in your quiet and comfortable room, your subconscious mind responds to the repeated conditioning. The thought . . . CONFIDENT EXPECTATION OF SUC-CESS . . . now takes possession. You no longer have to *think* it, but it seems to stay with you in the quiet darkness behind your lightly closed eyes. You seem almost to breathe the sure, secure feeling . . . CONFIDENT EXPECTATION OF SUCCESS . . . with your slow, relaxed breaths. At last conscious *thought* has become subconscious *feeling*.

I think you will smile a little, and sit there with closed eyes, smiling. At length a different person from the person who sat down will rise from that chair.

7. *Reinforce the confident expectation of success which is no longer a thought, but a deeply lived emotional feeling.*

As you may have realized by now, you did something like this, with a different technique, when you wrote your point-of-view letter. When the letter returned to you and you opened it and read it, you were flooded with the feeling of winning, the Will to Win, the victory values suddenly recalled to your thoughts and your feelings. The expectation of success is hardly any different; it is more *permanent* because it dwells deeper.

Now, to reinforce the confident expectation of success, once more read the point-of-view letter or letters you wrote to yourself; and read the success-factors that always have remained with you.

Also, go through the conditioning process in the quiet, comfortable room in the same way as before, twice a week or more often. Continue to look for and find the deep *feeling* that is expectation of success. And now you will find there is no further need for *words* in which to express what you feel. The confident expectation of success dwells within, radiating an influence that affects everything you do and everything you say. It may at times retreat before some onslaught of anger or sorrow, or even get temporarily put aside when you suffer plain physical exhaustion. But at a level far deeper than words, the confident expectation of success remains part of you; strong, deep, quiet, lasting.

8. *Know the signal that brings forth your expectation of success at any given moment.*

Once you have well formed that strongly conditioned *feeling,* once it is "clear as a bell and deep as a well," you can recall it in full strength by recalling the conditions under which you found it.

That is, when an emergency arises, or if at any time you feel the heavy pressure of adverse emotions, you can bring yourself back in physical feeling to your comfortable chair in your quiet and friendly room. This cannot be done until you have attained the full strength of the conditioning. Once you have that strength, you can bring yourself back to the room, so to speak. Doing it requires only five seconds or so. Even at a business meeting, men I have helped have found that nobody notices if they take two seconds in which to let their shoulders droop and their spines relax and let the tension flow out of their bodies while they look down at their memo pads, eyes half-closed in a momentary mental flight. For two or three seconds, every circumstance of the conditioning returns from recesses even beyond. You look up, then, once more quietly aglow with your self-confidence, with faith in yourself, with a confident expectation of *winning*.

But remember: The five-second "refresher course" is nothing more than that. First, the lesson must have been well learned! And also, the confident expectation of success in itself is but a foundation mood, a focal point, a central pivot, an effectuating agent for the mighty hidden potentials you have developed and for the specific skills and knowledge you need as building blocks for your success.

In fact, I do not believe it is possible for any man to hold a real, built-in expectation of success unless he has provided himself with what he needs to back up that expectation. Otherwise he is a phony, and he knows it, and he shows it.

Let us briefly review the several steps of the conditioning process. You should never have to stop and think about what to do next. Remember:

Your study of this book and your faithful performance of the Teleological Actions give you fertile soil in which to plant your expectation of success. This is the basic, underlying mood, or climate of emotion, that governs the lives of healthily successful men.

Faithfully, every day, you seat yourself in a comfortable chair in a comfortable room where you will not be disturbed and where you have no reason for hurry

128

or worry. (It is highly worthwhile to pay extra rent for that room if you must.)

Concentrating without strain upon the one thought— I AM GOING TO ATTAIN A CONFIDENT EX- PECTATION OF SUCCESS (or any words that mean the same thing to you)—you cast your thoughts briefly ahead and see yourself being successful. But most of all you concentrate—without strain, without anxiety, without effort—until the thought fills you and feels as natural as your long, slow breathing.

Without ever attempting to rush the process, and al- ways ready to try another day if that day's conditioning gets out of hand, you continue to remove yourself from the influences of the outer world for a little time each day, you continue conditioning yourself toward the confident expectation of success, of winning.

One day you find you are no longer thinking, but *feeling* the glow of confidence. The confident expecta- tion of success has now settled into the emotional part of your mind, the deepest part of your mind, the part that is most important.

You continue the conditioning process two or three times a week for some weeks. You also practice the way to find your expectation of success if ever it slips away from you or if ever you need to rally that great inward force in an emergency.

Can you give yourself any other emotion with the same conditioning process?

Yes, you can! And with practice you can give it to yourself al- most anywhere. I myself have used the process while seated in a taxi. The occasion was my daily visit to the bedside of a relation who was "dying hard." He had been a mean s.o.b. all his life, and with his death upon him he was letting loose one final howl of meanness. You visited him knowing you were going to get told how no-good you were and how he had hated you all his life. All my other relations wondered how I was able to visit Great-Uncle day after day and maintain a mood of patient cheerfulness until the Grim Reaper gathered him up. Or down. It wasn't that he had left me all his money; he had left nothing but debts. It was my conditioned mood of patient cheerfulness that stayed with me because I had set it up in my deepest emotional being.

In short, once you have conditioned yourself into living with the confident expectation of success, your mind is thenceforth confident that it can hold onto any other mood, or any other passing emotion. You can visit your dentist feeling quite friendly and relaxed. You can sit through a boring lecture (or party or dinner-with-speeches) without losing your poise. If you are a salesman, you can summon your enthusiasm afresh with every sale. If you ever face a desk piled high with an "impossible" amount of work, you can bypass any panic and quietly get organized and get it all done.

All of these merely implement your expectation of success in some particular manner!

Still, when you are on the spot, and you have not conditioned your basic mood of success, and you are not one of those few men to whom it comes without effort—you can always try the method I mentioned in the last chapter. There we met the young man who was afraid of his boss, so he visualized the boss without pants. As amusement came into the young man's mind, fear went out the window.

An unwanted emotion can always be pushed into nonexistence by a wanted emotion. Any dramatic gimmick is a great aid in this. It helps you ACT like the person you want to be, so you soon THINK and FEEL like the person you want to be.

The conditioning process, however, gets right down to the very bedrock matrix of emotion. It gives you and permanently holds for you a mood that settles down and becomes part of you. Deep. Safe. Sure!

TA: POSTGRADUATE CONDITIONING.

Once you have well and truly set up your confident expectation of success, I urge you strongly to go back to your chair and find another life-governing mood that is equally priceless.

You have dealt with the conditioning phrase: I HAVE A CONFIDENT EXPECTATION OF SUCCESS.

Now think back upon: *A merry heart doeth good like a medicine; a broken spirit drieth the bones.*

Change that quotation from the Bible into a conditioning phrase. Use your own words, but keep *merry heart* because it is so memorable and filled with meaning. Here's a good phrase: I AM CONSISTENTLY CHEERFUL AND OPTIMISTIC; MY HEART IS MERRY.

Now you have:

I HAVE A CONFIDENT EXPECTATION OF SUCCESS, and

I AM CONSISTENTLY CHEERFUL AND OPTIMISTIC; MY HEART IS MERRY.

You can see how the two phrases support each other and practically melt together in one grand over-all pattern of life!

And so, for postgraduate conditioning, return to your quiet room and your comfortable chair.

When you are relaxed, confident, ready to sit down, be seated.

Without anxiety, calmly, while you sit in a comfortable position with your eyes lightly closed . . . without forcing, without getting mentally on the edge of that chair . . . peacefully give yourself this second governing thought: I AM CONSISTENTLY CHEERFUL AND OPTIMISTIC; MY HEART IS MERRY.

Once again follow through with the entire process of conditioning.

Once again, just as gradually as before, the thought that implants a mood will approach the deep-lying state you desire. You will not know it, but it will be happening. One day it happens. I AM CONSISTENTLY CHEERFUL AND OPTIMISTIC; MY HEART IS MERRY becomes a basic and governing *feeling,* joined to your other basic and governing feeling: I HAVE A CONFIDENT EXPECTATION OF SUCCESS.

As the two melt together and forever after work together, you gain a mighty influence over achieving health-and-success, success-and-health: health enjoyed all the way up the ladder and all the more enjoyed when you reach the top.

Can I *guarantee* you will have success—health—healthful success? No. But I can and do most sincerely maintain that those two

131

phrases are natural focal points for the success-forces and health-forces within anyone's mind/body. They help you mightily toward becoming successful and attaining (or keeping) good health; they help you more mightily than you may ever have dreamed you could be helped.

One more caveat: I have said that I HAVE A CONFIDENT EXPECTATION OF SUCCESS means nothing if it is not backed up with the information and skills and seized opportunities that bring success. Just so does I AM CONSISTENTLY CHEERFUL AND OPTIMISTIC; MY HEART IS MERRY require a grounding in practices consistent with good health. What the health-phrase (as an attained permanent mood) does most strongly for you is to bulwark you against psychosomatic illness—the kind that a pattern of dismal, dark emotions seems to welcome in by the front door.

And you can win these mighty benefits not because you are a "reasoning" human being but because you have deep, vast emotions!

Do you accept yourself as an emotional being?

There is many a man who believes that it's always the other fellow who is swayed this way and that on tides of emotion, while *he* manages *his* life on a 99-per-cent-pure outpouring of logic and common sense.

No.

Maybe (if that is you) you kid yourself by ascribing "emotions" only to those who vividly display their emotions. But the driest stick of a man—one of those fellows who never shows a reaction to *anything*—is just as equally a bundle of health-and-success-making or health-and-success-breaking emotions. To borrow a phrase from the submariners: Our most important emotions run silent, run deep.

A psychotherapist mentioned to me that emotions are like a telescope. One person will look at a situation (interpret that particular reality) as though he looked through the eyepiece of a telescope, so that what he sees is bound to look large, nearby and perhaps threatening. Another person interprets the same situation as though he saw it through the reverse end of an emotion-telescope, so that to him it looks tiny, unimportant, far away.

Emotions. . . !

1. In the locker room at the golf club we always josh each other

132

about loud ties, way-out sports jackets and things of that sort. One day I josh my good friend George about a wild sweater he is wearing . . . and good ol' George positively snarls at me! Seems he is wearing a sweater he utterly dislikes, but it was hand-knit by his mother-in-law (whom he also utterly dislikes), who is coming to the club with his wife to have lunch with him. So, in addition to wearing the sweater, George is wearing a load of resentment.

2. A manufacturer ran a prize contest. The first prize was to be all the silver dollars the winner could shovel into a barrel within a certain number of minutes. The manufacturer, a muscular man, could shovel a bit more than six thousand dollars in that interval, so he budgeted the first prize at six thousand dollars. But the small woman who won the first prize shoveled almost eight thousand dollars into the barrel . . . because she knew she could keep every dollar she shoveled.

3. A transplanted Old World peasant, Nicholas, worked hard ten hours a day, poured good sour wine down his wrinkled throat, slept like a baby and didn't care that he had lost track of his age; he figured he was about sixty-four. Then a baptismal record turned up in the Old Country and he found out he was seventy-six. Nick faded; he stopped work and tottered about, aging before your eyes. Maybe he had found out too much about American retirement ages! But then it was discovered that the baptismal record covered an older cousin of Nick's who had the same name. Nick was only sixty-two! Within a week Nick felt fine and was building stone walls again.

4. It is only recently, as history goes, that schoolchildren have learned of the many advances in astronomy, mathematics, medicine and other fields that were made in ancient Islam. Ah, but Islam and Christian Europe were deadly enemies for many hundreds of years. We do not, in any epoch, on any scale, find it emotionally acceptable to give any credit to an enemy.

We do love ourselves, however; our native land; our children; our spouses; our own ethnic or religious or political groups; our *own.* That's very human, admirable in its way, and in fact quite necessary. But if you ever try to tell me that you love your own (anything) because it common-sensibly is *better,* I will tell you to grow up and be a man, my son. It doesn't have to be better or worse; it just has to be *yours,* and you love it.

No, it is not merely the other fellow who is swayed this way and that on tides of emotion. It is also *you*.

Action can create emotion.

The following short sequence is borrowed.* It is a bit of dialogue that occurs over and over in a class for salesmen. The instructor's words are set in regular type; the student's words are set in italics.

Do you want to feel enthusiastic?

Yes.

Then learn the self-motivator: To be enthusiastic, act enthusiastic. Now repeat this phrase.

To be enthusiastic, act enthusiastic.

Right! What is the key word in the affirmation?

Act.

That's right. Let's paraphrase the message and thus you will learn the principle and be able to relate and assimilate it into your own life. If you want to be sick, what do you do?

Act sick.

You're right. If you want to be melancholy, what do you do?

Act melancholy.

Right again! And if you want to be enthusiastic, what do you do?

To be enthusiastic, act enthusiastic.

That little sequence has a great deal to say! I will let it stand by itself, pausing only to remark, as every salesman knows, that emotions are highly transferable, and enthusiasm is surely the most transferable of all emotions.

Be glad you have emotions.

The emotional qualities that help a man succeed are, like success itself, a matter of degree.

Get to know any person who handles his life well and you will soon find out he is by no means entirely free of fear, anger, a touch of self-pity, even despair. It is his *general pattern* of emotion that is constructive, forward-marching, expectant of success. And by the same token, the "healthy" person is bound to have some little some-

* W. Clement Stone and Napoleon Hill, *Success Through a Positive Mental Attitude* (Englewood Cliffs, N. J., Prentice-Hall, Inc., 1960).

thing wrong with him now and then, but by and large he is healthy.

And notice in both cases that any negative, downgrading emotions that may be present only weigh lightly in those lives, while the other side of the scale is far more heavily freighted with courage, kindness, perseverance, enthusiasm, self-confidence, self-respect and just plain cheerfulness. And, yes, LOVE—which includes both the ability to love others and the ability to love yourself.

Be glad you have emotions! Rejoice that the circuits in your mind are not, like a computer's, limited to logic, but can take you soaring off into the boundless area of dreams. Be glad you have a conscience. Be glad you have a set of social values. Be glad you have a consciousness of *self,* and can appreciate the way in which your human mind—nature's crowning achievement—glows with ambitions, desires, needs, joys, fulfillments.

Know that without emotion you could not enjoy the wonderful world around you. The machine has limits but you have no set limits . . . neither in your ability to succeed nor in your ability to overcome obstacles and carry on. And also, it is only because you are an emotional being that you can judge the value of *improving yourself.* And know that the great spark activating your self-improvement is your emotional need to be better than you are.

Where we have been:
As you read another chapter, another unit in your constant buildup of your success-potential, check the mood you are in. The closer you find yourself to a confident expectation of success, the more strongly will your success-potential work in your behalf, like a friendly giant.

Successful men have a favorite mood—the confident expectation of success. This mood backs up every dream you dream; every effort you make in life. Also, a simple conditioning process can give you *expectation of success* as a mood that stays with you. Before you begin the conditioning process, have the steps firmly in mind:

Set aside the same time every day to go to the same room and sit in a comfortable chair to perform the conditioning process. Be sure you are removed from all outside distractions.

State your objective firmly. Hold it in mind without strain or anxiety. Your mind at first may wander, but soon you will hold the thought without effort.

One day the thought becomes deep emotional *feeling*. On that day the mood is rooted into your being. It does, however, require reinforcing, which is simple and interesting in itself. Then it will always respond to a signal whenever you want to renew the mood in its full, triumphant strength.

Remember, however, that no man can hold a deep-down confident expectation of success unless he backs it up with skills and knowledge. Once you are firmly conditioned to expecting success, take a "postgraduate" conditioning that helps you ward off the many ill-health influences that come from the wrong kind of emotions. The two conditionings work wonderfully together.

Emotions manifest themselves in many ways. Actions can build and change emotions. Realize you are an emotional being and be glad of it, for it is through your emotions that you fulfill yourself.

Where we are going:
As you will see in the next chapter, many of the problems of your life are rooted within yourself and can be solved by looking within yourself. Knowing this, you can apply definite problem-solving techniques that *work*.

9 Tackle Your Problems and Solve Them

The way you state a problem to yourself has a great deal to do with your finding a solution to that problem. Once you orient yourself toward the positive, you can find the hidden positive factor in almost any problem. If your goal really is to solve a problem, specific Teleological Actions put you into the right, problem-solving frame of mind and can make "impossible" problems almost find their own solution, as clear as crystal.

He was a cabinetmaker, a man of sixty with strong, sensitive hands. For more than twenty years he had worked in the same shop, but now the shop had burned down and he was out of a job.

He sighed, "It's a problem for an old man like me to get a job."

"Why is it a problem?"

"Why?" He was astonished at the question. "Nobody wants an old man."

"You have found that out?"

"Sure. Same story everywhere."

"Well, Ernie," I said, seeing that he needed a slight shaking up, "all you have really found out is this: When a man goes to see a shop boss, and that man sends out signals that say, 'I am nothing but an old man who is hopelessly looking for a job,' the shop boss doesn't see much reason to give him a job."

"But I *am* an old man."

"Are you?" Then I fired some questions at him. Was he in good health? Were his hands steady? Had he lost any of his hard-won skill? Did he have his own full kit of fine tools? To each question he answered *Yes* . . . and I noticed a rising note of excitement in each *Yes*.

"All right, then, Ernie! Let's play a game! I'm the shop boss and you have come to ask me for a job. Now go on out into the hall and then come back into this office like the man you are—like a solid old-timer, the kind that's worth his weight in gold these days, trustworthy, with high standards of craftsmanship, healthy, steady, well equipped, and with a good fifteen years of work in him if not more. Go on out there and come back and make me *eager* to hire you!"

Ernie did this. He got into the spirit of the thing, changing his negative approach into a positive approach before my eyes. I also had him make a list of his positive qualifications as a cabinetmaker, in detail, and the list came out strong. And here is the happy ending: Within two days, Ernie had a job.

What happened, really? A man had a problem that he interpreted in a certain way; that way, he was defeated. So he changed his interpretation and he took charge of the problem and solved it.

He also stopped saying *kick me.*

He also gathered and focused his expectation of success and found a Will to Win.

A problem is a circumstance of life; a real circumstance in most cases. *But the interpretation you put upon that problem is just as important as the problem itself—and often more important.*

Just about everything in life comes back to interpretation; negative or positive, mud-colored or rose-colored, high-flying or low-crawling or anywhere in between.

A problem presents a picture that seems inherently negative. *A mind that is keyed to success finds a way to turn that negative into a positive.*

The business that almost died aborning.

Richard Prentice Ettinger, Chairman of the Board of Prentice-Hall, Inc., almost saw his company die before it had fairly drawn its first breath.

The first Prentice-Hall book was a guide to federal taxes. No sooner did it come out of the bindery than the tax regulations were changed. Mr. Ettinger and his partner were in debt to the printer. They had to pay the debt, they had to get their new company rolling, and the only product they had to sell was an outdated book.

138

Negative enough? Negative enough to spell *irrevocable defeat* . . . if one wanted to see it that way.

But the men involved were positive-minded men. They looked for a way to turn the negative into a positive. They observed that although some of the information in their book had been made outdated, a good deal of the information was still sound.

The problem then was to find a way to update the several thousand copies of the book. Rewrite and reprint them? This was not practicable. But it *was* practicable to write a supplementary pamphlet giving the new regulations, and this pamphlet could be printed quickly, at low cost.

The books were sold along with a supplementary pamphlet. And —fortune favors the brave!—the separate pamphlet containing the newest "regs" turned out to be an excellent notion. Everyone liked it. It led eventually to the publication of a number of loose-leaf services, constantly updated, for accountants, lawyers, bankers and others. Prentice-Hall, that almost died aborning, now is a diversified publishing house with sales pushing up toward $100,000,000 a year.

Contrast this approach with the approach of the average Will to Lose character. Put a negative circumstance at his window and say Boo!—and all he wants to do is to find a hole and crawl into it and pull the hole in after him.

There is a positive angle somewhere.

The person who enjoys over-all success has not succeeded in *everything*. Every now and then on the way up he certainly tripped, maybe fell. But he always got up and got going because that always was his pattern, his interpretation, the signal that *he* heard life call to *him*.

Recently I read the results of a survey that covered more than thirty thousand men and women. The man who managed the survey was out to see what a defeat means to most people.

He found out. For the majority of those thirty thousand people, one and only one setback wed them to defeat. Having missed the positive angle at some critical point, they stopped believing that positive angles could ever go to work for them—if indeed they had ever really believed so in the first place.

Many a time, someone else says *You are defeated* and we do not stop to see that the signal comes from a defeatist. As an example of what can be done after someone else says *Give up,* consider the case of Arthur Decio. His father had a business in trailers—or mobile homes as we call them today—but the business had never flourished and eventually it fell flat on its face. Having lost all his savings in the business, the older man handed it over to his son. The younger Decio was then in his twenties. His father expected him to liquidate the business. What else was there to do?

What else was there to do? Look for the positive angle! First of all, Arthur Decio decided to give people what they wanted, which at that time was a small trailer easy to haul around. (His father had never bothered to find that out.) Also, the younger and more positive man found out that the "mobile home" market includes both a large proportion of young-marrieds and a large proportion of retired couples, so he aimed his new models' features and his advertising at precisely those groups. In short, certain people wanted certain kinds of trailers by the tens of thousands, and what more could a positive-minded businessman ask? The last I heard, Arthur Decio has made five million dollars out of a business that was about to go under.

I hark you back also to the able young man-in-the-right-job who sold me on renting that retail store. He turned my negatives into positives I simply had to accept, and solved a problem for both of us.

Somewhere there is a positive angle to just about any problem. *Know* there is a positive angle, keep your eyes wide open and suddenly you see it, standing tall as a signpost, pointing out the road on which *you* take charge.

Now that we have set up the over-all picture, we have some important procedures to fill in.

TA: DEFINE YOUR PROBLEM CAREFULLY; STATE EXACTLY WHAT HAS TO BE DONE.

The cabinetmaker at first stated his problem as: *Where in the world can I find someone kind enough to give an old man a job?* On those terms, his problem was a millstone around his neck. When

he was led to the far more positive restatement of his problem—
What is the best way to show myself to a prospective employer as a man whom it would be profitable to hire?—he was led straight into an interpretation of himself that got him a job.

How did the publisher take charge of his problem? Not by thinking: *My problem is how to get rid of a lot of outdated books.* When he said, expecting success: *What's the best way to compensate for the partial outdating of my otherwise excellent reference works?* he found that way.

The young man who was implicitly told, *Your problem is to get rid of the mobile home business and salvage what you can,* did not accept the transference of dismal, negative emotion. He saw his problem as merely that of building the right product for the right market; he did so, and roared ahead.

The even younger man who sold me on that hardware store could have stymied himself with a problem-interpretation such as: *How in the world can I put over that marginal store to an experienced man like J. K. Summerhill, who knows so much more about stores and merchandising than I do?* Rather, first in his own mind, then by gathering data to back himself up, he found *positives* he could sell. And even though I was ready, willing and able to ignore those positives, he didn't let me!

After you think you have defined your problem, challenge the definition.

Most definitions of a problem are really approaches to a definition. Keep on challenging your definitions. First of all, you have to weed out the merely glib ones that sound good, but are superficial. More importantly, as you go along asking yourself . . . *But is that the real problem?* . . . you cut through layers of emotional conditioning. Remember, for most of us, there are solutions to our problems that we would rather not see. Dig, however, and there they are.

Again, you may not find your problem's correct and positive solution until you have tried one or two or more solutions that were not correct. One cannot always see ahead with perfect clarity. The important interpretation to apply to a solution that proves itself wrong, is: *Okay, then, since I now know that approach is wrong, I know more than I did before and I am all the closer to the correct solution.*

Perhaps the most famous for-instance along these lines is the story of how Thomas Edison at last found a suitable filament for his new incandescent electric lamp. Some say he made ten thousand experiments that ended in failure; some say he made fifty thousand. Certainly he worked his way through thousands upon thousands of failures, knowing that each failure brought him closer to success.

Another story, rather a domestic one but with obvious implications in business and in several other kinds of human activity, is the story of the wife who remembered her mother too well.

A husband moved his wife and child to a new home in the suburbs. This wife had always been strangely dilatory about her household duties. She promised now to turn over a new leaf. But still, she consistently neglected a new but simple duty—she "never got around" to watering the lawn. At last she said the trouble lay in the nasty, heavy, black rubber hose she had to use.

The husband suggested getting her a nice, modern, light, clean plastic hose from The Big Little Store That Has Everything. She agreed to this and he told the boys in his commuter train that now he had solved *that* little problem. But he soon found he had not solved it because his wife still neglected to water the lawn!

One day at his office, the husband became angry and picked up his phone in a great rage, called his wife and told her to get out there and water the lawn. He came home and found she had indeed watered it.

"Dammit," he said, "do I have to make a long-distance call every time I want the lawn watered?"

The wife burst into tears. "Yes," she sobbed. "I just realized . . . I've been that way . . . all my life . . . I have to be told to do something . . . or I just don't do it."

This woman had been brought up at the mercy of a domineering mother. She was accustomed to acting upon Mother's stern direction; otherwise, how could anything turn out right? After three years of marriage she had made herself able to stumble through most of the motions of housework, but that bad old emotional block came through when she had to face a new problem, such as watering the lawn.

I am glad to say that once a counseling session brought the real problem into the open, it solved itself. The woman has found she can water the lawn after all because now she *knows* where the trouble began, and she can laugh at it.

Will you always find a solution to any problem?

The only honest answer is *No*. Now and then we meet a situation that nobody can do anything about. To quote the first part of an old Chinese saying: "You cannot stop the birds of prey from flying over your head." But on the other hand, there is a great deal you *can* do something about, and the person of basically optimistic nature *always* looks for that positive angle. And sometimes, in the looking, we find that the annoying birds are not out of reach after all. Which brings us to the complete saying: "You cannot stop the birds of prey from flying over your head, but you can stop them from building nests in your hair."

One of these days you may find a problem right in your hair and feel there *ought* to be a way around that negative circumstance. You try and you try, you feel you *honestly* try, but you cannot surmount it.

Then you must ask yourself a very significant question:

TA: ASK YOURSELF: "DO I REALLY WANT TO SOLVE THIS PROBLEM?"

As you saw a couple of chapters ago, many a person is sick because he gains something by being sick. Just so can one find he "cannot" solve a problem because the very existence of the problem offers some advantage to him.

A woman told me that her great problem was to get her straying husband to return. She said she had made desperate efforts to bring him home. When we examined her efforts, however, it became clear that each effort stopped short of the final drive that might have brought success. (Highly indicative of a Will to Lose. Over and over, Will to Lose characters point to the vast efforts they have made in order to attain some job or other goal; and time after time you find they stopped short of the final push that would have carried them over the top.)

As for this woman who, she said, wanted her straying husband to return: She didn't. Down in her deep emotional being, where her conscious mind could ignore the knowledge, she knew she was much better off if her ne'er-do-well spouse kept right on drinking, wenching and living far away. But she nursed her problem and kept it warm because (a) it reinforced her wish to appear respectable, in that trying to get one's husband to return was what she thought a "respectable" woman should do, and (b) she enjoyed the sympathy she received from her family and friends.

What is *your* continually unsolved problem?

Enter it here:——————————————————————

————————————————————————————————

What might be *your* reason for preferring to let it go unsolved? Enter it here:——————————————————————

————————————————————————————————

————————————————————————————————

It will help to read the following list of often-used reasons. If any one of them stops you cold—especially if it rouses defensive thoughts such as: "No, *I* couldn't be that silly!"—you have found a likely suspect. Give it a big black check mark.

( ) Your problem wins sympathy and attention you enjoy.
( ) Your problem serves to set you off from your neighbors; it makes you in some way a distinctive (even if unhappy) person.
( ) Your problem, if solved, would cut you loose from some childhood carry-over you cherish. (For example, the wife who would not water the lawn still wanted her mother to give her orders because in this she found a kind of security.)
( ) Your problem keeps you from facing another problem that might crop up if you solved the first one.
( ) Your problem enables you to control someone else.
( ) Your problem enables you to get even with somebody.

144

( ) Your problem enables you to evade a responsibility.
(You have to care for your widowed mother, so people just don't bother you with other matters. So you go on caring for your widowed mother even though she herself has said she would rather live in a modern, cheerful retirement home.)

There are endless combinations. Try a few on for size!

"King Solomon trouble."

You can't make an omelet without breaking eggs. And very often you can't solve a problem without hurting or bothering someone else.

This factor in itself is a problem. You see a solution to a problem, but someone has got to be hurt by it. King Solomon offered to cut a disputed baby in half, one side for each woman who said she was the baby's mother . . . but *you* shrink from the King Solomon approach.

So do I.

But when a problem continues indefinitely, then it is in charge of you, it is in charge of the other fellow, and everybody gets hurt.

The Teleological Action that follows is an evaluation process. It is slanted toward the solution of the many problems in which conflicting personal claims or personal rights have to be evaluated. Someone has to give in. Who? The more formal you make your evaluation of the problem, the more likely it is that your solution will be fair and just.

TA: FORMALLY EVALUATE THE ROLE OF OTHERS IN YOUR PROBLEM AND ITS SOLUTION.

The process will remind you of the "detective work" you did in searching out psychosomatic health-factors. This is good, since one process reinforces the other, and you may now find other clues about "problem people" who you never realized might be affecting your health.

You have arrived at the proper definition of the problem?

You have your pack of 3 x 5 file cards?

Take a number of cards equal to the number of persons involved in the problem . . . employees, family members, club members or whoever they may be.

Now take one more card. That one is for the person you forgot to include—yourself. Head each card with the name of an involved person. See yourself as just one more involved person.

Write the following information on *each* card, using extra cards if necessary. This takes some thought and some work. It is eminently worthwhile.

1. How and why is that person involved in the problem?

At this stage you may be agreeably surprised to find out that the person is not really involved; he has merely acted involved, or you have assumed he is involved. But if he is definitely involved, define his involvement with care. This includes yourself.

2. How will that person be affected by any solution to the problem that has suggested itself?

Here it is well to use auxiliary cards, one for each possible solution. Put each *solution* card next to each *person* card, one by one, and see how *solution* is going to react on *person*. (This process often suggests additional solutions.)

3. Make another run-through of all the person *cards and for each person ask: What* rights *has he in this matter?*

What rights has a parent? A child? An heir? A worker of *x* years' seniority? And does this person have rights that are real or merely assumed? And has he been asserting his rights, as compared to some less assertive person whose rights may nevertheless be just as strong?

4. Are trial solutions possible? A solution with an escape clause keyed to time, to the possibility of a future event or to some other similar factor?

And if a trial solution is possible, is it advisable? Might everyone be better off if the matter were settled right now?

Any of these points may lead you on into other investigations.

By and large it is a good idea to follow such leads. You may find yourself understanding for the first time just what makes someone tick. You may see the true significance of someone's pattern of action. You may come to realize you have been pushed around by some person; and you may come to realize that some person has been too shy to ask for help he needs.

Take time to look at yourself and at others.

Few of us give enough time to real analysis of ourselves and other people. You need not ever have taken a course in psychology to understand a great deal about people when you *try* to understand. It is just such a formal evaluation process as this that gives you a framework on which you may gradually hang a great deal of understanding. Knowledge is power, and knowledge about people is power of a particularly useful kind.

Follow any leads that may open, so long as you do not lose sight of your main problem. As the fire chief said to his men when they grew excessively interested in a new fire alarm system: "Don't forget, fellows, our main work is to put out fires."

So—you have a problem to solve, the solution has to hurt *somebody,* and you have taken a broad four-step procedure toward showing you who it is that has to give in.

It will be *somebody.* Somewhere along the way of those four steps, sometimes even at the first step, you will see through the tangle of conflicting claims. You will have your solution.

And then, *ouch!* You can depend on it; somebody, maybe several people will point out why your solution is simply *not fair.*

The best course to take is to say you know it is not 100 per cent fair, and if anyone cares to come back at you with a perfectly fair solution, you'll be glad to talk it over. Then go ahead and ask if anyone can show you why your solution was not the *fairest possible* under the circumstances.

You will find that you are the only one who knows the full depth and breadth of the circumstances. *This tells.* And when the shouting is over, decisions made in this manner are often accepted and *respected.* The people involved come to see they are dealing with a man who knows the answers.

"Have I known and solved a similar problem before?"

It's strange how often people will attack a problem, perhaps in worry and confusion, without stopping to remember they have tackled it and conquered it before.

The lists you made to help you write your point-of-view letters are essentially lists of problems you have tackled and conquered. Use those lists to "bring you back."

Often, if they will not remind you of an occasion on which you conquered the same problem, they may remind you of a problem-solving *method* you have not used in years.

Thus, a man who could not pay his business debts faced bankruptcy. He needed time, for he could see daylight ahead, but it would not be tomorrow's daylight or even next week's. His attorney and his accountant told him that nobody would give him any more time.

Now he remembered an occasion many years ago, before he'd gone into his own business, on which he had an argument with his boss. And he had won the argument, not by arguing, but merely by asking the boss to be patient till he straightened out a certain matter—which he did.

He sat quietly awhile, gathering his confidence. (See Chapter VIII.) Then he phoned each creditor in turn. He made no bones about his not having any money. He merely asked quietly if he might have more time. He said he was a man who preferred to pay his debts rather than go bankrupt and hurt the men to whom he owed money. Would they help him pay his debts, merely by giving him some time?

In every instance, he got the time he needed. He is solvent again, and his business reputation is terrific.

He solved his problem by remembering how he had solved a problem in the past. And often when you have not solved a problem that resembles your present problem, someone else has. Find out!

Deadlines and decisions.

One day I did a great service for a man by sending him to the movies.

He faced a business problem of considerable importance. He had

148

sweated with it, consulted experts, slept on it sleeplessly. He had even tried writing it out, sealing it into an envelope and keeping that envelope in the middle of his desk so that all day it got in his way, and he knew it would be in his way until he solved it.

I saw he had reached the point at which that problem had to be solved one way or the other or it would ruin him. Already he was terribly fatigued and twitching with anxiety.

I phoned a local movie and found out the main feature would start in half an hour and would be finished two hours later—at 4:15 P.M., as I recall.

"Go and see that movie," I said, "You'll get out at 4:15. It will take you, say, six or seven minutes to walk back to your office. Go and sit at your desk, knowing that at 4:25 P.M. you are going to come up with a solution to that problem . . . *either way.*"

"But how will I know I'm right?"

"I don't know if you will be right, but a fifty-fifty chance is mighty good odds. In any event, you will reach a decision. You'll stop being paralyzed. Your business can proceed again."

"Why a movie?"

"Because you can't look at a movie without thinking about what you are looking at. And I don't want you to think about that problem for at least two hours."

He went to the movie and when he came back to his desk he felt calm and strong. It often happens that way when one gets away from his problem for a while. He ripped open that sealed envelope and in red pencil printed his decision beneath the problem. Then he dictated a memo that nailed down the decision, and went home for a happy evening and a good night's sleep.

When you can't get a decision out of yourself in any other way, give yourself a deadline for decision. Then, till that deadline arrives, get your mind off the problem. Deep mind-forces help you. There is a great deal we do not know about the human mind, but we have found out some very good ways to make it *work*.

Man-brain, bird-brain.

I have invited you before to be glad you are human, and I invite you again. *You can learn by experience!* By problems! By difficulties! By mistakes!

There is a little bird called a junco we often see around during the winter. He is a seed-eater. You can watch how he flies to the top of a seed-bearing weed and bends it down with his weight. Then he can peck out a seed, which he does, and hops away and eats it. When he hops away, however, the weed springs back upright. So the junco flutters to its top again, bends it down and repeats the performance.

I find myself wondering how I can get it over to that poor bird-brain that it would be much more efficient to *keep* his weight on the bent-down weed while he ate one seed after another! But there you are—he's a bird and I'm a man. He can fly and I can't. But I, assuming a highly plural *I*, have built a civilization because I think constantly in terms of *improved method*.

Look at a junco, look at the far more intelligent dolphin, look at the intelligent and five-fingered ape, and see over and over that the mind you carry between your ears is fantastically far ahead of any other mind in nature. The ape has a certain amount of problem-solving ability. Compare his to yours!

Be glad you have problems! Where would we be, individually or as an entire human race, if we did not continually face problems and solve them? The more you know, the more you don't know. The more you don't know, the more you are going to find out.

I close with a thumping quotation from *The History and Present State of Discoveries Relating to Vision, Light and Colours,* by Joseph Priestley, published in London in 1772. Priestley was a father of modern chemistry. He also was a very canny observer of mankind.

> . . . every *doubt* implies some degree of *knowledge;* . . . it may be expected that the more knowledge we gain, the more doubts and difficulties we shall have; but still . . . we have reason to rejoice at every new difficulty that is started; because it informs us that more knowledge, and more advantage are yet unattained, and should serve to quicken our diligence in pursuit of them. . . .

How about that for turning a negative into a positive!

Where we have been:
A problem presents a picture that seems inherently negative; it

150

is trying to defeat you. When your mind is keyed to success, you find ways to turn negatives into positives. This worked with a man who needed a job; it worked with a man who was starting a business; it works for everyone.

As a survey showed, most people are ready to give up after one defeat. But, even after someone else advises you to give up, you still can often find the positive factor that gives you victory. Go back to the definition of your problem and challenge that definition. This makes you analyze the problem and more clearly see your own reaction to it. Also, make sure you really want to solve your problem. Many people gain something by allowing a problem to remain unsolved.

Formally evaluate the role of others in your problem and in its solution. Use file cards to show you how every other affected person is involved; how that person will be affected by each solution that presents itself. Trial solutions may do the trick. In the end, when you follow this process, you are bound to find a solution that is the fairest possible. You cannot please everybody, but your solution will be respected.

Make sure in all events that you use the problem-solving powers you know you possess, those your point-of-view letter brought into the open. When you cannot come to a decision, get your mind on other matters for a while, but set up a deadline for decision. And take note of your great human problem-solving power, which is ready and able to work for you if you will only let it.

Where we are going:
Your energy and your Will to Win are strongly connected with each other. The next chapter shows you where almost all fatigue comes from—and how to banish it with actions that build a dynamo of energy.

10 Find and Use Plenty of Energy

Some people seem to be born energetic, and so they have all the drive they need to carry them on to success and wealth. Others seem to be born tired, and fail. Yet nine-tenths of our energy output is governed by our emotions. You get signals to be tired, so you are tired. This chapter reveals an amazing truth about energy that makes every man his own energy-generator, no matter what his previous record has been. You can talk away your own energy; also talk fatigue (or energy) into others. Victory brings energy. Pleasure of any kind brings energy. The emotional basis of pleasure in your life has a great deal to do with your energy and drive and zest . . . and your energy is tied closely to all else that makes you prosperous.

You know the kind of person who becomes spectacularly tired. All knocked out, almost as though you had hit him on the head with a hammer. Ted was like that. At eleven every morning, he became utterly exhausted. About all he could do between eleven and noon—lunchtime—was to reach across his desk to answer his phone, and even then he would beg the caller to try him again after lunch.

In his energetic hours, Ted was a valuable worker. So his boss worried about him, and made sure the company bought him a thoroughgoing "physical." Ted was in fine health.

So it went, until daylight saving time arrived on the wings of spring. One night the maintenance staff set all the office clocks ahead. It happened that they neglected to change the clock that was in Ted's line of sight. The next morning, when the hands of that clock pointed to eleven, Ted sagged. He got that heavy feeling around the jaw and across the shoulders. His motions resembled those of the three-toed sloth that can take all day to move ten feet.

Suddenly he realized that all the people around him were getting up and going to lunch! It wasn't eleven o'clock; it was noon! Ted had worked right through the morning. He was bewildered. It had never happened before! But, as we pointed out to him later, he had simply missed a certain signal he had come to depend upon—a signal that said, *It's time to be tired.*

Most of us go through life with some sort of signal that tells us when to get tired. I am talking here about *emotional* signals, not the signals induced by true physical fatigue. I am talking about the emotional signals that account for nine-tenths of tiredness, and maybe more.

Some signals are quite definite, as was Ted's eleven o'clock call to collapse. Such signals are often rooted in a deeper matter. Ted, for example, did have some midmorning fatigue. It would have gone away in a few minutes if he had let it. But he subconsciously exaggerated it, and he made a dependable routine out of it, as a form of protest. Deep down, Ted was utterly bored with his job.

Other signals come from broader sources. They still are signals —we'll be talking about them—and they still say: *Put yourself into a state of fatigue.* For, when people droop and drag; when work seems impossible to perform; when play, too, is abandoned because of lack of energy; when many a chance for enjoyment and many a chance for achievement go out the window . . . rarely is it because of prolonged effort that brings on unavoidable fatigue. People are far more likely to get tired because of some factor that runs through their lives.

Some *emotional* factor. *People get tired of what is happening to them.*

Cross-examine your fatigue.

You don't have to be a giant of performance in order to keep yourself far ahead of most others—and have far more money to spend. You do have to have some edge in various directions we have explored, and surely, the possession of energy is an "edge"

153

that vastly affects everything else. So cross-examine your own fatigue and pin down your own get-tired signals. And thus, knowing yourself, you can improve yourself. Because your fatigue is a life-handicap you largely "wish" upon yourself, you can stop a lot of that kind of wishing.

Watch for the connection between tiredness and defeat; between energy and victory.

Here comes George, striding into his office after a week's business trip. He greets everyone jovially, rips into his accumulated mail. He prepares a report, briskly sets up everything he needs for his appointments the next day and goes home whistling, announcing he is going to take out the old lady for a night on the town.

And, on another occasion, here comes George, creeping into his office after a week's business trip. "Darned traveling wears you out," he groans. He tries to take care of his mail but can only look at it in dull annoyance.

The first trip was successful! The second trip was a failure, a defeat. The first trip signaled to George's deep-down emotional stratum, *That was great!* so he felt great and full of energy. The second trip signaled, *That was a flop,* so he felt and acted like a flop.

This is classic. I don't think anyone is completely immune to at least a short time of energy-loss when his emotions have taken a beating.

The Will to Lose character, therefore, takes a consistent beating —so consistent he hardly knows it any more; he is merely beaten down and that is that. After a while he doesn't even *need* energy.

When your basic pattern is SUCCESS, however, you snap back quickly. An executive told me: "I can see that in a man—if he's got an energy in him that cancels out any goof he makes and puts him right back up there where he belongs."

Concerning your own energy, quick-check the mechanical details:

Do you eat sensibly? Do you get enough sleep? (And do you know that many people who claim they are energetic on very little sleep are either on their way to a breakdown, or are cat-nappers, or are just plain fakers?) Do you avoid exhausting yourself with a physical output in sports or otherwise that may simply be beyond what is good for you? In short, can you reasonably say you *should* be energetic—yet you are not?

Then think back upon that matter of *confident expectation of success.* And add this statement to the record: *Energetic people are successful; successful people are energetic.*

Sometimes energy is quiet energy, but it is there, getting that man's work done right and all his affairs attended to without constant fatigue dragging him down and befuddling his senses. *Energetic people are successful; successful people are energetic.*

And when that act-think-feel-act cycle is working for you, not against you, you can briefly go punch-drunk from a hard punch, but you *always* snap your actions, your thoughts and your feelings right back where they ought to be.

TA: CHECK AND SEE IF YOU SUFFER THE TIREDNESS OF INDECISION.

Watch for the *energy of decision* and the *energy-drain of indecision.*

You recall the man I mentioned in the last chapter, whom I sent to the movies? As I made clear, he suffered from terrible fatigue. But his decision, once made, acted as a tonic. Your best tonics always come from within yourself.

A decision gets you past a barrier in your life. It brings you up and over a heavy hump of doubt.

Most doubt is self-doubt.

Both the decisive man and the indecisive man may be observed muttering to themselves . . . balancing the pros and cons that lead to a decision. Let nothing I say about the value of being decisive deny the value of gathering the data you need, weighing it and sifting it. Any decision should be based on good information, and I have seen success-attuned men wait for good information while others, in a panic, rushed ahead, making decisions that first of all were not respected and most of all turned out to be shortsighted in the extreme.

155

What you will *not* see in a basic winner is the gnawing agony of doubt when he has to make a decision. You'll see it in a loser, however, all the time. For a winner, making a decision is nothing more than a mental process; and if some penalty will follow his decision if it was wrong, why, that's life. But for a loser, making a decision is a form of destructive torture, all the worse because his agonizing doubt is *self*-doubt. He does not merely admit that something can go wrong; he *knows* it *will* go wrong; he may even subconsciously help matters to go all awry because he is a loser.

Over and over I see this dreadfulness of indecision in the people I counsel. Their minds tend to be mare's nests of unresolved questions, evaded issues, confrontations with fact put off and dreaded and dreaded. Are they tired? They practically stagger.

The chapter on handling problems can help you make decisions and make good decisions. And the more good decisions you make, the more confidence you will have that you *can* make good decisions. Again, look for clues in your Will to Win letter and its associated lists. You are always better than you think!

And always, when you have to make a decision, remember: " 'Tis better to have loved and lost than never to have loved at all."

Meaning: 'Tis better to live a life that contains some honest mistakes and some honest successes than to have nothing happen on either side of the ledger.

You can bat .400—that's six failures out of ten tries—and still play in the Big Leagues.

The most terrible, damaging score a man can make in life is: *no hits, no runs, no errors.*

Here is another basis for "get tired" signals—with or without a clock to watch:

TA: CHECK AND SEE IF YOU SUFFER THE TIREDNESS OF BOREDOM.

When I was in college I had classmates whose fathers sent them plenty of money. I worked my way through. Summers were my bonanza time. I'd take a job at a huge mountain hotel, waiting on tables and rassling luggage. I made a thousand dollars, some summers. In mid-September I'd come home with a week or two to go before classes began. And I'd rush around to find my classmates,

156

see what parties were going on, see who wanted to go boating or play tennis. I was all set up for fun.

But my friends, who had loafed all summer, my rich friends by now were terribly bored and so, so tired. They couldn't understand why I was so energetic.

Wherein we may see two lessons: One: Play is most valuable as a contrast to work. Two: All play and no work makes Jack a dull boy.

Do you get bored (and tired) on your vacations?

That's a fighting question. Maybe it annoys people because they know they *do* get bored when they are supposed to be enjoying themselves. Bored and tired . . . as natural a combination as bread and butter.

I speak now of the couples or families who go away on Pop's two-week vacation to some resort on the shore or in the hills. Basically this is a wonderful idea. And if Pop wants to do absolutely nothing for a couple of days after he arrives, this may be just what he needs.

But then what happens? To paraphrase what a number of hotel men have told me, "The first week of vacation, the average couple is very happy and peppy. The second week is what we call the quarrel week. It's like—the honeymoon's over, the fights start."

The vacationers begin to grow restless, bored, therefore quarrelsome and *tired*. This fatigue gets itself blamed on "your tiredness catching up on you," one of those grains of truth that gets magnified out of all proportion to the fact.

Don't let me talk you out of any kind of vacation or any length of vacation you really enjoy! Life is meant to be enjoyed. Only be honest in handling the feeling that you *must* enjoy yourself. As one man told me back in my college days: "Buddy, let me give you some advice. When you're married, don't let your wife tell you it's your duty to take any particular length of vacation. When you've had enough, dammit, tell her it's time to go home."

I am proud to say now, decades later, that I have been instrumental in getting some companies to change their viewpoint on vacations. They give their people one week in summer and one week in winter, more or less. It works out very well.

Vacations are like eating. You feel better if you quit while you still could squeeze in a little more.

Having a job is not in itself a cure for boredom and the fatigue of boredom.

There is the job. And there is You, viewing your job through your own interpretation of "job," as we have discussed it.

Anyone in management knows the meaning if not the exact words of Parkinson's Law: *Work expands to fill the time made available for its completion.*

As Shakespeare remarked: *'Tis true 'tis pity; and pity 'tis 'tis true.* I daresay half of those who hold jobs are goof-offs. So you never have to look far to find someone who is expanding his work to fill the time available. And, by the same token, you don't have to look far to find a man with a job who is bored and tired. Anyone who drags out his work drags out his personality.

Take note of those who fit vast amounts of work into even a short working day. By and large, they work with zing and zip. You may say: "But they were energetic people to begin with." Not always. As with the woman who shoveled all those silver dollars, consider the energy of *incentive.*

I have seen many a desk worker, bench worker, salesman, executive, pull himself out of tired boredom and respond to a pile of work that simply had to be done in short order—especially when it was to his own advantage to get that work done!

I have seen an entire shipping department get itself dedicated to the holy slowdown, accompanied by such waves of fatigued boredness that you could almost see the waves rolling through the warehouse. And I have seen those same men, who had been grumbling they worked as hard as they could, more than double their output and go home ready for star performances in the bowling league. What did it? Merely a new piecework incentive system: the more books you packed, the more you were paid.

Also *variety* helps to combat boredom. The coffee break has value not merely as a period of stretching one's legs and nourishing oneself, but also as a short period of gossip.

I recall being in a factory, trying to sell something to the pur-

158

chasing agent, when gongs went off and there were cries of "Fire!" The fire was minor and was extinguished in a few minutes. Several hundred people meanwhile went down two flights of fire escapes and back. In short, they had a little break from routine. It was notable how brisk and energetic they were for some hours afterward, and how much work got done.

What is boredom? It fits right in with the general description of emotionally induced tiredness: *You are tired of what is happening to you.* I believe this is inevitable with some people. I don't think it is inevitable with you, because you are reading this book. If you are bored at your job, you are not doing your best work, you are not doing all you can for yourself, you are not taking charge of your life; you are letting circumstances take charge of you. Now is the time to do something about it!

TA: DO YOU CALL ANY OF THESE ANTI-ENERGY SIGNALS?

Harvey Carey, a public relations expert, trained his entire staff in *the mechanisms with which people affect each other*. To understand how to affect thousands or millions of minds, Harvey used to say, you've got to understand how one mind affects the mind next to it. This is well said.

Think of how having lunch with a cheerful person brightens you; how a sourpuss makes your own mouth turn down. Think of how you feel when *A* confidently invites you to, "Come on, let's get the ball rolling," as compared to *B,* who says, "Can't we put off that lousy job?"

Notice that what is transferred from mind to mind is not merely an emotion; with the emotion goes the *effect* of the emotion. The energy content of the emotion!

Find your pencil and get ready to check any or all of the following items. Where you may recognize yourself, salute yourself with a good, big check mark. Where you may recognize someone else and his get-tired (discouraged, bored, beat) influence upon you, jot that person's initials next to the item. Notice, too, that there also is a positive column—the one to the right. Check on that side, with equal honesty, for yourself or for the other person.

By the way: Don't neglect to come back to any and all of the check lists and other lists in this book. A year from now, looking them over, you will want to change some of the checks you made. You will be a different person. Or, now or later, you will find it interesting and very helpful to jot your own notes in the margins of the pages.

Now here is the double check list. Do *you* call any of these signals? Do you know someone who does? (If so, you win great aid in judging his worth and his potential; in assessing his influence in your life.)

Words and attitudes that kill energy

Words and attitudes that generate energy

You come home from work groaning, "I'm worn out," or some such phrase. You make quite a drama out of your fatigue; everybody has to cater to you and be concerned about you. This kills energy.

You may not come home fresh as a daisy, but you de-emphasize your tiredness with a cheerful expression of interest in what is going on around the house. You may take a rest, but you do not require your household to revolve around you as an exhausted hero. This generates energy.

Facing any circumstance of defeat—say a contract lost or the discovery that your new model is a flop—you announce over-all defeat. You say, "We're licked" or, "That kills us." This kills energy.

You report a defeat in the spirit of: "Well, we can't hit every ball that's pitched. Now let's get ready to hit the next one over the fence." Moving away from any connotation of frustration or unworthiness, you generate energy.

You are a kill-joy. With a "What's the use?" or "You call that fun?" you pull both effort and enjoyment down to a common appearance of futility. This kills energy.

Believing that life was meant to be enjoyed, you show enthusiasm for your own goals and appreciation for the goals of others (even the fun-goals). This generates energy.

160

You say you really have plenty of energy, but you can't find the right way in which to show it; that is, you can't find a target worthy of setting up as a goal. This apparently superior attitude really indicates inferiority and a fear of competition. Not only does it kill energy; it does not allow energy to be born.

Having a Will to Win and goals to gain, you go all-out toward your own fulfillment. This generates energy.

You are wedded to indecision so strongly that you hate to let a decision stand. You insist on endless reviews and post-mortems—"Maybe we're all wrong" —so that action gets stopped whenever you can stop it. This kills energy.

You make as sure as you can that you are right. Then you go ahead. This generates energy.

You sneer at enthusiasm. Perhaps being a quiet type (which will never prevent you from being successful) you consider any expression of emotion as childish, any cheer as sophomoric. This kills energy.

You naturally vocalize and dramatize your enthusiasm for what you are doing. This generates energy.

Which items did you check?

Think about them.

Think about what you are going to *do* about them.

Relate them to all else we have said about tiredness and energy; about boredom, about defeat, about indecision, about signals for fatigue.

And do this:

TA: WHEN SOMEONE SIGNALS A NEGATIVE TO YOU, SIGNAL A POSITIVE RIGHT BACK AT HIM.

You feel and think the way you ACT. So act cheerful, energetic, forward-going—and you will feel the part!

161

When you hear, "What a blow!" respond with, "We have plenty of ammunition left."

When you hear, "What's the use?" respond with, "We won't know till we try, so let's start trying and give it all we've got."

This sounds oversimple. Maybe it sounds corny to your ear. But let me assure you that many a discouraged person *wants* someone to give him a different kind of signal. He simply cannot summon his own resources, and he is grateful—he admires you—if he borrows yours. And then, having announced your energetic approach, you *will* be energetic!

Anyone who handles a crew of salesmen knows this phenomenon. Specifically, a man gets discouraged with his progress and comes to you and says, "Give me a pep talk, will you? Give it to me so that it sinks in!"

The ability of a mind to communicate feelings to another mind or other minds is so great and so deep, it can hardly be comprehended in its full, awesome power. And while words are our usual vehicle of thought, the communication can be well accomplished without words, especially when that other mind is particularly receptive.

A special warning for fathers.

Take note of the first two items on the preceding check list. They deal with the man who comes home and makes certain signals to his family . . . acts out a certain role. Where do you stand? Ask yourself if you signal: *I'm bushed—I've had it—now it's up to the rest of you to take care of me.* (Along with this go heavy implications of: *Look at the mess I have made of myself for YOUR sakes.)* Or do you come home to an exchange of cheerful greetings? And perhaps a short rest before dinner that is just a short rest and not a drama of despair?

Take a good look at yourself as you enter your own front door. If your favorite role is Poor Tired Pop—with your family required to attend you with pillows and aspirins and guilty concern—you are doing harm all around. And there is one particular, helpless target for the damage you do.

What about Junior? His young mind receives impressions that mold his life. Already he senses that some day he will grow up and have a job and bring home money, just like Pop. Fine. But what else? If your favorite role is Poor Tired Pop, you show him that when *he* comes home from work, *he* must put on a big show of fatigue and make everybody wait on him. You are telling your son to *expect* to be helplessly tired. And with his impressionable young mind so instructed, so that the instruction sinks deep into his sub-conscious, he will be helplessly tired no matter what, with an entire atmosphere of fatigue ready-installed to shadow his entire existence.

Fathers and mothers give their children all kinds of advice. Better than your advice is your example. Don't merely tell; *show* your children how to be cheerful, energetic, friendly, loving, capable of enjoyment, INTERESTED IN BEING ALL-ALIVE. Do this, and you may do more for them than you could do with any conceivable sum of money.

Energy generates energy.

I have been leading up to that one strong and strongly founded statement. *Energy generates energy.*

To be enthusiastic, act enthusiastic.

To be melancholy, act melancholy.

To feel the way you think the way you act, act that way.

And so, to be energetic, *act* energetic. Because energy generates energy. At first you have to push yourself, make a conscious effort. But in a while you find your output of energy becoming an acquired conditioning; you definitely feel better when you are putting out mental or physical energy or both for a really large proportion of each day. At length—I do not say overnight—at length the energetic way of life simply becomes *your* way of life, with enormous benefit to the way you act, the way you think and the way you feel, and a vast increase in your success power. *Energetic people are successful; successful people are energetic.* The mind can take charge of the body. And the body can take charge of the mind.

Your emotions, your glands and your energy.

I am sure you know you have a number of glands located in strategic places in your body. The pituitary and other glands act as our regulators; as our thermostats and alarm systems, you might say. They obtain a good part of their effect by regulating the flow of digestive juices and other secretions, and by guarding—and sometimes altering—the blood's chemical balance.

Now let us enter upon a constructive byway. In what I just said rests the entire physical rationale of: *A merry heart doeth good like a medicine; a broken spirit drieth the bones.*

Take the all-too-inclusive emotion of *fear*. We no longer are cave men, and our emergencies are more likely to be caused by bankers than by saber-toothed tigers. Still, we know fear in many forms.

Now, in a real physical emergency—a threat to your life—your heart beats faster, you breathe hard, you may sweat, your muscles tighten, your lips draw back in an instinctive animal-like grimace. All these manifestations signal that your body has made itself ready to meet the desperate emergency. You are suddenly much stronger and much faster than you generally are because suddenly you are ready to fight or ready to run.

What happens inside is that the mind signals EMERGENCY, and the glands, alerted, pour energy-giving adrenalin into your bloodstream. Thus it was when the cave man met the tiger. Thus it can be with you in, say, a driving emergency, when you save your life by becoming extra-fast in your reactions.

We automatically respond to EMERGENCY, and when the emergency is over, our mind/bodies return to their usual state. A real emergency is a temporary condition. *Temporary*. But now let us see what happens when we live in a long-continued state of alarm, anxiety, apprehension; not only in a sort of low-key condition of emergency but also looking forward to more and more of the same.

Say you have gone half your lifetime in dread of losing your job. (Cave men did not have such worries.) Then for half your lifetime you suffer, not the fear of instant annihilation, but still a fear, an aching knowledge that you are threatened. Your mind will still react on an instinctual level. Your glands will still get a signal to get you ready to meet the threat. The effect will not be so great as it would be if you met a tiger; but still there is an effect. There is an alteration in your bloodstream and other alterations elsewhere in the body . . . quite tolerable when they are temporary . . . quite harmful when they go on and on. And there is nothing temporary about a dread that lasts half a lifetime.

Thus a long-continued state of apprehension—very common to man in his man-made world—does no man any good. It will tell on your health. It "drieth the bones."

I have simplified a very complex matter, but I hope you get the point. Now let us go back to the main thread of our discussion, which is *energy generates energy*.

Your glands also respond healthfully to natural stimulation.

You may know someone who takes glandular extracts to stimulate his energy. Glandular extracts also are used to make up for deficiencies of other sorts, and in their place I daresay they do a deal of good.

On the energy side, however, my medical advisers tell me that few people need anything so drastic. Moreover, when the fatigue-drag is rooted in the emotions, where most fatigue keeps its roots, no medicine will prevail for long over the mind, and continued dosing may put you into a very unsafe condition.

Now, suppose your glands really are a bit sluggish. You can still force yourself into action. But would you always have to go on forcing yourself to put out energy . . . to do what does *not* come naturally, so to speak? Or . . . will energy *really* generate energy?

Here is the answer. I have put it together from information gathered from several competent sources. Yet, as I have said, I am a pragmatic so-and-so; I have to see things *work*. I assure you that the phenomenon I describe I have seen *at work* with men and women in a wide variety of jobs and a wide range of ages. Here it is:

If you really have a sluggish physical make-up and you push yourself into action, the body will gradually respond to the demands you make upon it. With an output of energy you stimulate everything in your body that governs your output of energy.

Millions of tired people think they need more rest; what they really need is the stimulation of action. They need a mind keyed to action and a body in action to get the mind all the more keyed to action.

It is *action*—energy output—that acts as your natural, healthful gland stimulator. Gradually the glands, muscles, sinews and organs become accustomed to working harder. So does the heart become accustomed to meeting the moderate extra demand. *Energy generates energy.* Not only are successful people energetic, but also by being energetic they help themselves to be more and more energetic. Of course there is a natural, healthful stopping point, but it is fantastically far beyond the stopping point that the lazy wish upon themselves.

Energy generates energy. The mind takes charge of the body, and the body takes charge of the mind as well. By thinking, we make ourselves act, and by action we make ourselves think. Which comes first? I go to my research files and I read:

> . . . the argument over which comes first, thinking or doing, is as bitter as the long-debated question concerning which came first, the chicken or the egg. . . .
> In the case of producing changes in any significant area of behavior, thinking and doing are inextricably interwoven. Progress in the two must proceed not only simultaneously but in close relationship to each other.*

Also I turn to my King James Bible and read (Proverbs 23:5): "As he thinketh in his heart, so is he."

Finally, having looked at energy from several related angles . . . having shown you that energy to help you achieve and enjoy is waiting to be released—by *you*—in the subtle apparatus you carry above your neck . . . I am going to end with an angle on energy that sounds rather simple. It *is* simple. But it sums up much that is important to know about your energy and your entire life. I suggest you read it carefully, then sit back and think a bit.

As energy generates energy, so does PLEASURE generate energy.

The youngster who can play vigorously for hours is all beat when

* Ross L. Neagley and N. Dean Evans, *Handbook for Effective Supervision of Instruction* (Englewood Cliffs, N. J., Prentice-Hall, Inc., 1964), p. 114.

his mother enforces upon him a short trip to the corner grocery.

Good news (or a raise in pay or a tight poker hand well played or a favorable report on your chest X ray) makes you feel like a million dollars. Bad news . . . but you know how bad news makes you feel.

Or you go shopping and can't find what you want, and come home exhausted and grumpy. Then you go out the next day and find the absolutely best buy in town in office space or fishing tackle, and wow!

Again we may use George, met earlier in this chapter, as a symbol of the energy that comes from pleasure and the pepless feeling that comes from lack of pleasure . . . in this case, a fruitless business trip, a defeat.

These are easy-to-see examples. The principle applies as well in every sort of complicated affair. But let's keep it simple, and go another simple step further:

You are sitting around bored and bone-tired on a rainy night and someone says, "Let's go see the high-school kids do Gilbert and Sullivan." You say, "I'm too all-in, I'm not dressed, and what's the use of getting wet?" But eventually, grumbling, you go. You enjoy the show, you recognize your neighbor's son behind his make-up, during the intermission you join the sing-along, you chat with people you haven't seen for some time . . . and you come home whistling. You may even get some dance music on the radio to work off your excess energy before going to bed.

Now, what happened here? You had no energy (and no particular reason to get into action and generate energy). But at length you allowed yourself to have pleasure. And in the attainment of pleasure you attained energy; it's as simple and as profound as that.

May we say, then, that in the pursuit of pleasure lies the path to energy and so the path to all the benefits of energy?

Yes, this is a fair statement . . . provided you put it on one side of the scale and balance the other side with an equivalent weight of good judgment.

All play and no work makes Jack a dull boy because *play* is *pleasure* only when it remains play. When play becomes a way of life, the adult has returned to a childish level and so may expect to become bored with such a way of living.

But when your play is truly pleasure, then the energy you put

167

into it is a particularly effective builder of *more* energy—truly as though the body took delight in the mind's delight.

What about your work? Can your work be a pleasure? We have gone at some length into this question; we have seen that your work, in its broadest aspects, should be a pleasure if it is to give you plenty of *worthwhile* reward . . . that is, plenty of money without ulcers.

Certainly your home life should carry a long, strong pattern of pleasure, day by day . . . and your nights, I hope, in a loved one's arms.

Your social life should be a pleasure; and there you have vast categories of activity. And in the final analysis, your life inside your own skin, your relations with your own self-image . . . this too should be a pleasure!

Well, I have set up so many sources you can mine for pleasure, I've almost made it seem as though pleasure itself could become a bore.

Fortunately, life is sufficiently various and demanding and often unjust, and human beings are sufficiently selfish and complex, that we cannot feel pleasure all of the time. Perhaps we'd all go insane if we did.

No, you are going to go through life merely with measures of pleasure; and when you attain a long-desired pleasure, you are going to find some little fly in the ointment—like, say, income tax. *But the principle remains.* In the pursuit of pleasure *does* lie the path to energy and thus to all the benefits of energy. And I use the phrase *pursuit of pleasure* to stir you up, to make you ask yourself if it sounds sinful to you, and if so, why.

The pursuit of pleasure is not sinful unless you make it so.

The world is full of people who are afraid of pleasure; they do not believe they are entitled to it. You can hear them make excuses for not enjoying themselves, no matter how ripe the conditions for enjoyment may be. They are "always upset" about something, generally something big and permanently troublesome, like the international situation. Without implying that it is unworthy to concern oneself with large issues, I still invite you to notice how these and similar issues serve as a constant *rationale against enjoyment*. People who *do* something about large issues, and *do* something about the injustices of the world, generally are people who also can let go and have fun, and then come back with new energy to the business at hand.

The confident expectation of pleasure is akin to the confident expectation of success.

In your confident expectation of success you know you have found no impermeable armor that keeps any failure or defeat from coming through; you know there is no such thing. Rather, with *success* as the norm of your emotional being you can handle setbacks and get going again; an occasional defeat is only the exception that proves the success rule.

So it is when you have a confident expectation of pleasure—a deep belief in yourself as a person who can and does enjoy life. Still you are going to know *dis*pleasure, surely hardly a day without it. But you handle it. And all the while, down there in the very matrix of your mind stays the foundation upon which, in a moment, you rebuild your zest and pleasure.

Zest and pleasure.

Success and zest and pleasure in success and zest that brings more pleasure.

Energy and zest and pleasure and good health and good wealth and the ability to enjoy God's good earth and the life you live . . . no one of these qualities exists without all the others. Thus a consideration of energy touches upon many other qualities; and as we consider all the other qualities, energy comes along to bring them all home.

Where we have been:
Fatigue may be physical, but most of us go through life obeying some emotion-rooted signal that tells us to be tired. We really get tired of our patterns of life; we are fatigued by what is happening to us.

Cross-examine your fatigue. Watch for the connection between tiredness and defeat, energy and victory. Note how the Will to Lose character tends to be the pepless type. Energetic people are successful; successful people are energetic.

Do you suffer the tiredness of indecision? A winner makes a

169

decision without torturing himself. A loser wears himself out with the conflicts of his decision. Losers often grow afraid to try, so their score in life becomes "no hits, no runs, no errors."

Do you suffer the tiredness of boredom? Even play can turn into boredom when you do nothing but play. Many people get tired when on vacation because their vacations are so long and boring. Spaced-out, short vacations often are the best kind. You also can be bored and tired on your job if you have no motivation to work energetically.

Do you call certain anti-energy signals? Change them to positive, energy-arousing, *go* signals. Note the terrific power of feelings to transfer themselves to others. Fathers can pass on to their children a climate of fatigue that haunts them all their lives.

Energy generates energy. The glands respond to activity by getting you ready for more activity. To be energetic, act energetic. And as energy generates energy, so does pleasure generate energy. In the appreciation of pleasure—constructively handled—lies the lifetime secret of energy; and energy, health, success, wealth, and zest for life all go hand in hand.

Where we are going:
The last chapter of TAKE CHARGE OF YOUR LIFE wraps up certain key factors involved in taking charge of *yourself*. You see reasons why anyone can find excuses for being a failure, and you see once and for all that anyone who really wants success can find the success of his dearest dreams.

11 You Can Be Sovereign of Yourself

Take charge of the routines that are so much a part of you, and you may find they need to be changed in order to give full expression to the best part. Change your routine way of reacting to certain people and you can change your entire life. You and the child you used to be are still the same person, but childhood influences will not hold you back unless you believe they will. All of us build our lives on the same basic human setup. All of us are prisoners of our Will to Lose if we want to be—or, with our own minds, we set ourselves free and the Will to Win becomes triumphant.

I once had a boss who kept a large pile of papers on one corner of his desk. Oh, that was an impressive pile of papers! And it always was neatly squared-off, for he was a neat man with a neat mind; if he was not successful, that is another story.

The papers sat formidably on the boss's desk in an advertising agency where I was a copywriter. That neat heap was our frustration and our despair. We'd bring in our brain-children and the boss would say, "Ah-hmmm," and put our neatly typed sheets at the bottom of the pile. Into the bottom of that pile went all our copy, along with letters to be answered, bills to be paid and everything else that lives its life on paper.

The boss's system was to work his way through the pile of papers, from the top toward the bottom. Of course he never reached the bottom; there always was a new bottom. If any of us copywriters or the copy chief or the controller or any of the account men needed fast action on some piece of paper that had gotten into that pile—it was murder. We almost had to submit affidavits to prove our papers should be dug out and attended to. The boss got so *bothered* when he had to do anything out of order. Let him work his way from the top of the heap toward the bottom . . . it was his way of doing things.

Maybe it's *your* way of doing things. Maybe you have made several millions because you take charge of your career, you take charge of your self-respect, you take charge of your Will to Win . . . and a pile of papers on the corner of your desk, constantly added to at the bottom, is simply the way you like best.

Actually, some very successful men like that system. THERE IS NOTHING WRONG WITH THE SYSTEM. It all depends on how you handle it. Which means, really, it all depends on *you*.

Who was the real boss—the man or his papers?

In the case of my long-ago boss (whose advertising agency went bankrupt) he wasn't really the boss. His pile of papers was the boss. *It* bossed *him*. Although he had some good creative ideas, he was miserably afraid of making a mistake. He was also frantically neat, because—as he would say rather too earnestly—keeping things neat is the only way to keep yourself from balling things up. (It *is* a help, but—)

Chances are this man's parents put an exaggerated value on his keeping his toys in order. Or perhaps he had been so badly punished for leaving things around that he still connected disorder with pain. Also, looking back, I think he was yet another one of those people whose parents got him to believe that everything he did was done wrong. That shows! . . . and it *hurts your life* until you realize it and realize you can rise above it.

So, as we consider a large pile of papers on a man's desk—a pile of papers representing his work and at least part of his fortune— we assign no inherent merit to that pile of papers and we assign no inherent demerit.

We see it generically. It is a habit, a routine, a fixed way of doing things. Well, we raise no objections to this. Routines are useful. They do get work done.

But here is the question: If you habitually keep a pile of papers

172

on the corner of your desk, or if you habitually follow any other routine or habit . . . does that routine or habit really do something useful for you? Or does it boss you? . . . even kick you? To say it another way: Have you deliberately fixed upon that routine or habit; or have you been driven to it by your inward emotions, so that your routine is really an acting-out of some tension within yourself?

Suppose it is the latter. And suppose you come to realize that your routine is not so much a means of being efficient as it is a reflection of something out of adjustment in the inward YOU. And suppose, then, you ask yourself what would happen if you deliberately changed that routine; switched right around to performing the same functions in a different manner, as though by a different YOU.

I can tell you. In fact, I've been telling you for about ten-elevenths of this book. If you firmly, consistently take goal-directed action—*Teleological Action*—you can change the way you are. When you habitually substitute another kind of action for your present way of doing things (which.includes your way of thinking about things) you can make the new way of action/thought as natural to you as was the old . . . not merely because you practice it . . . but also because your subconscious mind changes, adjusts, accepts, the new view.

One human-nature message can be replaced by another.

Human nature is not permanent! Rather, think of your deepest personality as though it were a tape recording you play over and over. But this tape recording can be erased by another recording made right on top of it, so that the new and more beneficial recording becomes the one you play over and over.

Up to this point I have given you specific Teleological Actions that of their very nature take hold of the deepest part of the mind and slant it toward health and prosperity. We are still on the same path. Here, however, I introduce a somewhat random element. I shall suggest certain areas in which you can make changes in your routines; but you will have to find your own changes and methods.

Look anywhere in your life. Change any routine you can change without doing damage. That is the seemingly random element. What I want you to see and feel, as you go along, is that it is not so random after all.

Sensitized as you are by now to the vast and happy possibilities of improving yourself, you know it requires changing yourself, and you know many ways in which your enlightened self-interest requires that you change. Since our routines, habits, action-ruts, are ways in which we express our inner selves, a change in a routine shakes up the inner self. That is what you are after!

And again, as in searching out psychosomatic health-factors, you will find that certain routines resist changing. They should be all the more suspect for it.

The very least a change of routine can do for you is possibly to show you a better way of doing things. The very most it can do for you is quite impossible to calculate.

We'll begin with your business life. My suggestions are intended mostly as take-off points for your own ideas. When you find a routine you follow (and you'll find plenty!), check it out for its inherent value. Insist on knowing whether your routine is really worthwhile *of itself,* or whether it is riding your back like the Old Man of the Sea.

TA: LOOK FOR ROUTINES IN YOUR BUSINESS LIFE, AND MAKE CHANGES, AS THE FOLLOWING ITEMS MAY SUGGEST.

Your routine when you handle your mail: Do you answer each letter right after you've opened it? Read all your mail through before answering? Get your secretary to open and unfold your mail (or merely slit open the envelopes), or not touch your mail at all?

Your routine when you answer a letter: Do you dictate? To a machine? To a girl? Do you insist on typing your own letters? Do you get out letters without delay? Is answering your mail your worst headache?

Your routine when you set up appointments: In rapid-fire order? With time between appointments? Does your schedule of appointments habitually reach far ahead? Is your schedule improvised day by day? When you visit another man's office, are you habitually early? On time? Late?

174

Your lunchtime routine: Is your lunch hour an extension of your business hours? A time of relaxation? Do you lunch alone? Do you seek out others, and if so, whom?

Your desk-top routine: What is on your desk most of the time?

Your routine approach with customers or clients: Friendly? Stand-offish? Strict as regards your performance and/or theirs? Undemanding?

Your routine when dealing with subordinates: Think.

Your routine when dealing with superiors: Think.

Your routine at business meetings: Think.

We have explored the effect of one's habitual approach when looking for a new job. You saw how revealing was the cabinet-maker's self-image, and how he showed that self-image (as we all do). And how he used the simplest kind of action to change his approach, and got his job. Your routine when you look for a job applies at *any* level of pay or position. As Dale Carnegie said: "When you see a man well placed and well paid, you can tell in the man himself how he got there."

Let's look back at *how you handle your mail.* A man who was feeling the strain of his responsibilities as head of a big printing firm told me he always had answered his letters as he read them— zip-zip-zip—a model of efficiency, he thought. The trouble was, he had afterthoughts. When he stopped to cross-examine his way of answering letters, he realized how many letters he called back from the mail room, or wished he had been able to call back before they were mailed. (No help to one's peace of mind.) He then made himself read all through his mail and then go back to the first letter to answer it. Meanwhile, he found, his subconscious mind had been at work, lining up what he really wanted to say. He realized his so-called efficiency had been nothing but a tense impatience to "get it over with." He saw this pattern as it showed itself in other ways. He made himself slow down, and got more work done and done better; and he now feels a great deal better.

Another man prided himself on being always available to his subordinates. Then, after closing time, at last uninterrupted, he caught up on his work. This gave him *real* fatigue, all the worse because of the emotional element involved . . . wondering all day when in *hell* he was going to get things done. He changed his routine. He set up a time in the morning and a time in the afternoon when he did not open his door to anyone. He, too, does better and feels better.

A salesman, proud of his ability to make friends (nothing wrong with that!), made friends with every receptionist in every office he visited. When he finally determined not to spend so much time "kibitzing" with the girls, he found out that his overtalkativeness had been a handicap to him. When a prospective customer came from his inner office to greet this salesman, and found him hanging over the receptionist's desk, there was an instantaneous bad impression. The salesman still makes friends, but with briefer conversations. He knows now why he lost some sales. His income has gone up.

Meetings show a good deal about the men who attend them. A man I counseled had great ideas, but he said he found it very difficult to speak up. What was his routine when he entered the meeting room? Invariably he took a seat at the far end of the table from the company president. I suggested he take a seat right next to the president, that he even get in early so he could be sure of getting such a seat. He found that a man in a front seat is *expected* to speak up. He noticed the company president automatically looked at him to see what he had to say. So he fulfilled the image someone gave him to live up to; he spoke. And was listened to. And spoke again. And is now on the rise, well on the way to a success that was long overdue.

As Emerson said, "Do the thing and you will have the power." Sometimes you have to trick yourself into doing the thing!

Maybe your job is such that your mail is better answered in zip-zip-zip fashion. Maybe company meetings have no place in your success. Fine! Success lies far less in any circumstance or any routine or habit than in the significance of the procedure to YOU.

Don't get all tensed up with watching yourself.

All this procedure of changing your routines can be taken as a game. Change your routine "for fun," and see what happens. When you discover yourself enmeshed in a routine, laugh at yourself; it is just as easy as frowning at yourself.

176

Notice that truly successful men generally have the gift of laughter, and they don't mind if they laugh *at themselves* now and then. The all-out neurotic is notable for having no sense of humor.

Thomas Edison, one of our truly great self-made Americans, was very deaf. He used a hearing aid—a clumsy device in his day. My father, who knew Edison, tells me that the Wizard of Menlo Park had a way of switching his hearing aid on and off while you talked to him. It was quite a game, a relaxing element, and put a chuckle into every conversation. Note that Edison thought nothing of calling attention to his own disability—making fun of himself. It takes a man who is big inside to do that.

Watch your routines tolerantly. Change them without being frantic about it. All you are guilty of is being human.

TA: LOOK FOR AREAS OUTSIDE OF BUSINESS IN WHICH TO CHANGE YOUR ROUTINES.

Find a different way to go to work.
Read a different newspaper for at least a month.
Attend meetings of groups with which you disagree.
Go to the other fellow's church.
These may seem like trifling matters. But *any* change of routine gives you, at the very least, different scenery, whether physical or mental. You may go right back to your own way of doing things, and in such matters you probably will. But you will have been somewhere else for a while and you go back refreshed. The well-known phrase "travel is broadening" applies even to this kind of travel.

At the same time, whatever may be the nature of your job or your family life or your social life, pay strong attention to a certain type of change of routine that is highly inclusive and very important.

TA: CHANGE THE WAY YOU HABITUALLY REACT TO ANY PERSON WHO HABITUALLY PUTS YOU ON THE DEFENSIVE.

Have we been here before? We *have* been here before. This is *very* important in taking charge of yourself.

Begin by taking note of some continued dis-ease you routinely suffer in the presence of another person. This, too, is a routine, and a distinctly emotion-oriented routine.

Often it signals itself in some particularly odd manner. I shall give you just one story to show you how strangely the element of fear creeps into human relations.

A youngish, intelligent man was the son of a small merchant, and had been brought up in rooms behind the family store. His father had been a small merchant because he was small inside. As only one of several indexes to his father's personality, the son related that the father would never accept a check from anybody, no matter how long he had known that person.

So run the vagaries of the human psyche that the son, now in his late twenties, could hardly bring himself to use his own checking account! He expected to have his checks questioned, and he cringed at the prospect. I asked him if there was some particular instance in which he would prefer to pay by check and was completely entitled to pay by check, but did not because he felt intimidated. Yes, he said, he would greatly prefer to pay his rent ($140) by check instead of cash. But he had gotten started on paying every month in cash to his apartment house superintendent, a rather mean soul *who reminded him of his father*. Now he didn't seem able to give the man a check.

So I made him do it. First I rehearsed him. On the first of the following month, he rang the superintendent's doorbell. This is how it went:

> Superintendent: "What's this? I always get cash from you."
> Our man (*cheerfully*): "That's right, up till now."
> Superintendent: "Well, I dunno about taking a check."
> Our man (*pleasantly*): "Why not?"
> Superintendent: "How do I know this check is good?"
> *Our man smiles and waits.*
> Superintendent (*now on the defensive, for he knows, as tyrants know, that most of his strength lies in his bluster*): "Well, I mean—uh—I've got to protect the owner—I mean, because you always pay in cash . . ."

Our man (*tolerantly*): "You mean I used to pay in cash. But I guess I grow wiser as I grow older. 'Night. Regards to the missus." (*Walks away.*)

It still was some time before our man felt at ease in giving out his perfectly good checks to the superintendent and to others; but he does it now. The important thing about this one breaking of a long-established routine was that it provided the *breakthrough*. Our habits and routines can reflect inner patterns that shadow everything we do. Break the pattern at one point and it begins to go away everywhere. Our man now pays $700 a month in rent, which he now can well afford, and that is not the only difference in his life. The main difference is in him. He has stopped retreating. He is as pleasant and cheerful as ever; but in addition he shows his self-respect.

Does someone always make you go on the defensive?

Look, and look honestly, and you may find you habitually go on the defensive with someone in your life. Go back and read again the chapter on taking charge of your self-respect, and you'll refresh yourself on exactly what I mean. Break the *defensive* routine you set up with certain people, and you can break your defensive pattern all around. Does that mean becoming offensive, constantly attacking? You know it doesn't! It means carrying on your human relations with boss, secretary, wife, child, parent, landlord, tenant, customer, debtor, creditor, anybody, on a level of complete equality.

Also go back and reread the story about the copy cub who always took the attitude that his work was bad. Again you will see another slant on this same problem: We respect the other person's skill and knowledge that may be superior to ours, but still, the only valid approach between two human beings is one of absolute *essential* equality.

So you can find out from whom you are retreating no matter who the person may be.

Remember that short remark: "I grow wiser as I grow older." It applies at any age; it is a peacemaker; it does not put any blame upon the other fellow. And it leaves you with your victory!

You and the child you used to be are still the same person.

What about this matter of a man's fearing to pay by check because he had been intimidated by his father's mistrust of checks? And what about this matter of my old boss's showing the result of some damn-fool disciplining he had had in his childhood? Must we go through life as the victims of whatever bad influences were exerted upon us in our early years?

There is no straight *yes* or *no* answer. We can say symbolically, "The child is father to the man"; or we can say realistically, "You and the child you used to be are still the same person." And we mean that there is a large tendency for childhood influences to carry over. But only a tendency!

You are wiser than the child you used to be. You are stronger, you are far more experienced; and unlike the child you have escaped the power of your parents and have acquired great power over *yourself*. With few and fairly obvious exceptions, every one of us is inherently capable of taking effective, constructive charge of himself.

We know it is highly possible to improve your health without ever knowing what made you sick. Just so is it highly possible to rise above the failure-influences in your life even if you never find out where they came from in the first place. And if anywhere in this book or anywhere in life you find the means to make your own grand and glorious march out of the shadows and into the golden sunlight . . . take it as your due and keep looking *forward*. You are entirely welcome to use my own philosophy: *What works, works!* Should you find that even the simple outward procedures of Teleological Action send you high on a soaring flight of achievement, with new health and vigor, a vast new fortune and great joy in life —without your ever seeing why you spent many years being chained to the ground—don't spoil your success by doubting and wondering. Go!

With all that, let me make clear that *most* men do not make the great take-off until they come to know a good deal about themselves. Toward this end I have included a good deal of *inward* Teleological Action. Such is the check list (coming up) that shows you much about your parents, yourself and the influences of your childhood. It is based on the fact that by and large those people improve themselves best who know themselves best.

As you go through this check list, where you see reference to "parent" or "parents," take the terms to include anyone who may have influenced your early childhood. Also take heed of the semantic implications that go along with such words as *father, mother, parent* and the like. Such words mean neither *wise* nor *unwise,* neither *good* nor *bad,* neither *saint* nor *sinner.*

TA: READ THIS CHECK LIST CAREFULLY BY PAIRS OF ITEMS, RIGHT AND LEFT. CHECK ANY ITEM THAT GIVES YOU A SHOCK OF RECOGNITION.

If this is the way you are

This is the childhood influence that may have made you that way

You demand that others give in to you. Even in unimportant matters, you must have your own way.

A parent made it his main duty to give you what you wanted. You may have played this submissive parent against the other, stronger parent.

You can't get interested in what interests most other people. The same applies to your goals; you tend to forget them. Life may seem pleasant but nevertheless a bore. You also may be too fat or show other signs of overindulgence.

Since your father or mother or both stuffed you with presents, food and treats, you never had to ask for anything. You never connected *reward* with *effort* or felt you had to cooperate with others for your own good. (Often it is a grandparent who overwhelms a child with gifts and goodies.)

You'd rather be ordered to do something than be a self-starter. You like to have a strict boss. Now and then, in futile rebellion, you may be "too tired to work" or otherwise useless, perhaps by means of self-induced illness.

You had coercive parents who overwhelmed you with directions and exerted a high degree of control. (Some kids run away. In this connection, note that any coercion upon a child can result in rebellion or overcompensation.)

You drive yourself, forever must do better than anyone else. This urge may override friendships and the amenities of marriage.

Perfectionist parents made you feel that their love and acceptance depended on your performing beyond your age level. In your household, *average* meant *poor*. Perhaps you were continually compared with some sibling who outsmarted you. (Sometimes an overcompensation results in a teen-ager's taking to his bed to avoid competition, or otherwise going inert.)

You may try to make friends but you end up lonely, and often you are anxious in an unfocused way. You feel you need group identification, yet you shy away from it.

At least one of your parents neglected you. Divorce, long illness and absence in a hospital, death —all may correspond to neglect. Or a parent may show his or her dislike for parenthood, or substitute expensive toys for indispensable mother/father love. (The neglected child often joins a gang to compensate.)

You pay exaggerated attention to your body's functions and sensations. Generally you are tired, often you are ill or at least you find something physical to complain about. Your physician may be unable to find anything really wrong with you, but still you feel you require a lot of doctoring.

You grew up in the midst of people who expected ill-health. Perhaps the household was dominated by a sick person. Your bodily organs and functions were made into a fetish. Not only could you avoid unpleasant duties by getting a bellyache, but also you got sympathy and "understanding."

You set a low value on yourself and your abilities. You tend to keep company with others of the same ilk, who help you "hate the world," or you may sink into a dull forget-I-ever-existed state.

You were made to feel you were an unneeded, unwanted child. You may have been compared unfavorably with a reputedly "more loving" sibling.

You kick yourself around and consider yourself as being bad or at least unworthy. Unless you are working terribly hard at some punishing job, you feel guilty. You also feel guilty at accepting pleasure, terribly guilty if you find yourself pursuing pleasure. You may join some religious or other group that is highly dedicated and overzealous.

Punishment was an outlet for your parents' tensions and you got too much of it. Your parents set up too many actions as being little short of crimes. You got used to being "wrong" and "bad." (Your parents probably thought they were bending the twig toward virtue. Often such efforts to make saints result in criminals. The bent twig snaps back!)

You have some overweening area of worry or fear, such as money, health, or even a terrible concern with what the neighbors will think.

Your parents or your dominant parent worried about the same thing.

How did you get along?

That check list is strong meat. Perhaps you were shaken and startled. Perhaps old memories really hurt.

And perhaps you wonder why the author of this book, who prides himself on having shown the road to success to so many men, wants to get you shaken up. Well, I saved that check list for this final chapter because it presents you with a confrontation with yourself—and you can handle it. There is hardly a person who does not recognize himself somewhere in that check list.

So you face a moment of truth. And you discover whether, at such a confrontation, you tend to unleash your Will to Lose and let it run riot . . . or whether you run up the bold flag of your Will to Win that is just as much a part of you and just as natural.

That check list of childhood influences, set before one who is a victim of his Will to Lose, can have a negatively reinforcing effect. Right there is all the rationale for losing that you'll ever need. See, you are the helpless victim of your upbringing! You've *had* it.

But: When I show this list to people who take charge of their own Will to Win, I get a pause . . . perhaps a frown . . . and then a nod of understanding.

Of course, that is simply the way it is. We have parents. We have childhoods. We have other influences exerted upon us by all kinds of people. In short, we are humans who live among humans.

The great message of that check list is: *You are human, along with all that being human means.*

You had parents. You had a childhood.

You went to school. You got a job.

You have friends, you know love, you know pleasure, you know displeasure, you quarrel, you have bad times and you have good times, you have personal obligations and business obligations, you have plans and goals, you have a store of experience, you pay your taxes, you have money and you want more, you know you are not going to live forever, you know it doesn't pay to act as though you were going to die tomorrow. . . .

And when you look around at the other fellow, you see he is the mirror image of yourself.

Neither you nor he has to be a special kind of person. But you and he do have to exert control over the events of your life, stop worrying over any rusty old chains that may seem to hamper you, shrug them off and start marching.

Success waits for all kinds of men who come from all kinds of backgrounds, who have all kinds of basic personalities, all kinds of tastes acquired Lord-knows-how, all kinds of ways of doing things acquired Lord-knows-where. And still all the drives of your life can be slanted and beveled away from fear and toward courage, away from failure and toward the golden success that waits for any man who knows it is up to *him* to make *himself* successful.

The story of the king who was put in prison.

This is our last story. It is a very old one, a parable that I believe comes out of ancient Babylon.

Once there was a king, monarch of all he surveyed. But he was not a good monarch. He meant well, but he was negative; he held back his kingdom and made it poor and dismal because he couldn't seem to get the knack of thinking ahead, looking ahead, moving ahead. His subjects grumbled, "Our king is a do-nothing," but still, he was the king and they were helpless, and they suffered.

Now the king had an adviser, a philosopher who generally stayed

184

in the background, who gave good advice but was ignored. One day, however, the philosopher took the king by the ear, knocked off his crown, snatched away his scepter, hauled him down the street to the prison, thrust him into a gloomy dungeon and slammed shut the heavy iron door. And there the king stayed, unkempt and miserable, with a loaf of bread each day and a dim candle like any other prisoner, to howl at the injustice of his fate.

(How long did the king stay in the dungeon? It depends on who lives the parable, for the king is you and the philosopher is the deepest part of your mind that will work wonders for you if you let it.)

So the king stayed in the dungeon . . . held behind the great iron door . . .

Until, one day, he remembered something the philosopher had said about taking action to get what you want. So he kicked at the great iron door . . . and it opened a crack. And he pushed, and the great iron door creaked, and shed rust, and opened a few inches. And now the king put his weight onto that door that had held him in misery, and the door swung wide open. In the dark shadows, he went up the damp stone steps, and the shadows grew lighter and lighter until sunlight fell upon his head. Where were the outer gates of the prison; where were the jailers and the turnkey? Gone. Nobody stopped him as he walked out into the streets of his capital city.

And now a happy citizen shouted, "Our king walks toward his palace with a firm step!" and came running with new robes to replace the dirty old ones. And another happy citizen shouted, "Our king has the light of victory in his eye!" and came running to give the king a new scepter.

Thus equipped, and accompanied by cheering throngs, the king returned to his palace and walked straight to the throne room. There stood the philosopher, holding the crown. "Our king henceforth will lead us to greater and greater joy and good fortune, for no longer will he cripple his own abilities," said the philosopher, and as the king returned to his throne, the philosopher restored the crown to his head. And privately whispered: "The door is never locked. We are never prisoners save as our own minds make it so."

If you'd like it in more modern language, you have it right at the beginning of this book, in the Foreword:

185

Here is a man named X . . . at the age of fifty he earns an apprentice's pay . . . he's tired, he's bitter . . . his wife loyally makes the most of what he brings home, but they know what they are missing. Get to know this type of man and you'll find he never did anything about TAKING CHARGE of his attitudes, his abilities or any other part of his life. At fifty he still doesn't know that a circumstance that means *defeat* to one man can mean *victory* to another. If he never learns how to TAKE CHARGE of his life, he'll never eat anything more than crumbs at life's table.

And here is a man named Y. Week after week he pockets ten times the amount of X's salary, likes his work, takes plenty of vacations and feels fit as a fiddle. Watch him park a handsome car in front of the handsomest house on the block. Watch him walk in with a handsome present for his wife, and later welcome his friends to a plenteous dinner and a bright social evening. *Y is no smarter than X,* but Y did something about his "fate" and his "luck" in life. Y has no basic gift or talent that X doesn't have, but Y *took charge* and won instead of losing. This type of man enjoys a big, juicy slice of pie at life's table.

That is the way anybody can see it happening all around him if he *looks.* That is the way action sways thought and thought sways feeling and feeling sways action and it *works.*

The end of my book is your new beginning.

Following this chapter you will find an appendix that repeats and briefly summarizes every one of the tested and proved Teleological Actions that help you take charge of your life.

From time to time go through the list. See which Actions take hold most strongly in your mind and make you know you should perform them again. Check the list when you need a check-up on what it takes to make a good decision, what it takes to make your work worth more than your pay, how we are made and unmade by our emotions, and so forth.

Give it a little time. After many years of going in the wrong direction (if that has been your trouble), it does take a little time to get reorganized and off to a great new start. Yet it will never be an entirely new start, for your entire life-experience now goes to work on *your* side.

Calmly think about yourself: what you are, where you are going, what is the best way for YOU to get there. It is not only in action and in feeling, but also in thought that we keep our progress active, rewarding and dynamic. Get used to thinking through what you are doing, and you instantly raise yourself above the level of your fellows.

George Bernard Shaw bowing us to the wings: "Few people think more than once or twice a year. I have made an international reputation for myself by thinking once or twice a week."

Where have we been?

A long way. But your life always is yours to make wonderful. It is *never* too late to improve yourself.

Where are you going?

To the heights of success—success along with a brimming measure of good health, love and life-enjoyment.

Whatever you face in life is yours to interpret as you will, yours to handle as you will. Know, therefore, that your life is not so much the measure of the circumstances that come your way as it is the measure of you as a man.

Appendix

A listing, by chapters, of all the Teleological Actions set up in this book to guide you toward better, happier, far more prosperous living:

I. TAKE FIRM CONTROL OF YOUR WILL TO WIN

1. *Make a list of any occasions in your life in which you were a winner.* Big success or small success, it makes no difference. Only remind your inner self of how many times you have been a winner, and you build up the feeling of winning that can do so much for you.
2. *Add specific win-factors to your list.* Now you set down the specific winning qualities you showed on so many occasions; qualities you can apply in many ways; qualities that always stay with you.
3. *Write a point-of-view letter.* Writing as though to a stranger, you speak as one who knows a great deal of victory in his life. Telling nothing but the truth, you mail the letter to the convinced stranger who is YOU.

II. GET A GRIP ON YOUR SELF-RESPECT

4. *Stop saying KICK ME in any service situation.* Realizing that we all serve each other, you get rid of any apology in words or manner when you require service, and never neglect getting any service you are entitled to.
5. *Show that you respect the work you do.* No matter how new at a job you may be, you do your best and expect your work to be respected. Accepting correction from

the expert, you surrender none of the essential worthiness you know is in your nature.

6. *Practice saying "I like it that way."* You stop living in retreat by showing that your simple preference is sufficient reason for many of your simple actions—and say "I like it that way" both on the cup-of-coffee level and on the trampler level.

7. *Hold back on explanations and apologies.* You meet the world knowing that a small margin for error helps us all get along, apology is rarely needed, and most apologies only disclose the man who is in retreat.

III. ENERGIZE YOUR FULL GOAL-WINNING POWER

8. *Decide what you want your money to buy for you.* Small dreams do not have the power to stir you. Set up a big dream, put it in writing, make sure it is truly your own and fulfills your full victory-mantled image of yourself.

9. *Set up a Golden Goal File.* You set up and maintain a file in which your Golden Goal becomes real, develops many facets, and can often spark you into action that brings you immediate money benefit.

10. *Set up an Interim Goal File.* Interim goals are money-*earning* goals, planned for the near future, handled in full detail in a file you keep alive—for once your goals are full and real, goal-winning ideas flock to your mind.

11. *X-ray your favorite "handicap" and see if it isn't a loser's limp.* Lack of education, supposed lack of intelligence, lack of "good breaks" and other loser's limps go out the window when your Will to Win takes over. You make your own "breaks," create your own luck.

IV. MASTER OTHER PEOPLE'S MINDS

12. *Take an emotional self-interest quiz.* You put yourself "in the shoes" of several people in various situations and see that an appeal to their emotions plus an appeal to their specific self-interest gives you charge of their minds.

13. *Check the emotional self-interest in good advertisements.* We all "sell" in one way or another. Good advertise-

ments are the quintessence of persuasion through emotional self-interest—but use every *take-charge* technique with honesty and good judgment, for some of them are dynamite.

14. *Know and use certain powerful human-nature levers.* Just a few "prime movers" become powerful tools in getting what you want from others, winning arguments by not arguing, getting your way yet keeping your friends.

V. COMMAND YOUR OWN CAREER—I: Finding the Right Job

15. *Check certain key items that show if you have YOUR right job.* You feel at home in your job, you feel all-alive, your job arouses and focuses your Will to Win, and above all you work like a "pro" at YOUR right job whether you run your own company or work for someone else.

16. *Consider key items that affect the man in business for himself.* "To thine own self be true" in deciding whether you want your own business and in preparing for it. You know that if you go into business you should go all the way, do it right, if you expect its considerable profit.

17. *Take three good aptitude tests.* When all three agree on half a dozen facts about yourself, that is the real YOU. Remember there are many kinds of jobs and somewhere your own best job waits to magnify your earning power.

VI. COMMAND YOUR OWN CAREER—II: Working With a Will to Win

18. *Print the following words on a file card: I AM GOING TO KEEP THE LEVEL OF MY WORK ABOVE THE LEVEL OF MY PAY.* This motto becomes the solid framework of your soaring job success, with a tremendous dynamic toward making you think, feel and act at the top of your talents.

19. *Tell some routine worker about your motto and watch his reaction.* The average man will tell you that you are

cheating yourself, but you know it is the other way around; you are making sure that your pay and position are always catching up to you.

20. *KNOW your present job; DO your present job.* As part of your bedrock probity you do any job as well as you can, thus building your skills and job attitudes and getting you ready to proceed with victory after victory, up the ladder.

21. *Identify any special opportunity your present job may offer.* Doing this, you can move onward and upward into a different type of work, or onto a higher level of the same type of work. Both approaches have success-power.

22. *When you see the opportunity you want to exploit, do justice to it.* Learn what you have to know to hold the higher job, and make sure that as soon as you get it you can take hold of it for all it is worth.

23. *See your complete picture for advancement.* Learn about your company, its products, its markets, its competition. Show your awareness of what goes on—on an executive level.

24. *Make yourself a man who knows the answers.* Use the six great question-forming words, Who, What, Where, When, Why and How, to synthesize experience in your own mind and to get to know the "answers" at the level you want to reach.

25. *Keep your own kind of company.* Both failure and success attitudes transfer themselves from mind to mind. Make your general norm the company of successful men, imbued with the Will to Win, whom you can find at any level of income—always moving up.

VII. BUILD YOUR MOST BASIC AID TO HEALTH

26. *Set up a rogues' gallery of your ailments and choose a suspect.* Proceeding from the great saying, "A merry heart doeth good like a medicine; a broken spirit drieth the bones," search out your dismal, damaging emotions that may have a drastic effect upon your health.

27. *Look for a motivating person or circumstance for your psychosomatic ailment.* You may gain something by

having a health problem! Look for clues at home, at your work, among circumstances that occur every day or periodically.

28. *Review the suspect list you have set up on handy cards.* One or two of your cards may hold your attention, and thus reveal you have found the cause of your ill-health— even though it may be distressing to find out.

29. *Deliberately change some emotional reaction.* You can laugh at what makes you angry, and soon the laugh feels natural and there is no room for anger. Fear, too, can be displaced with an emotion of your choice. Reality may be beyond changing; but your interpretation of reality can always be changed.

VIII. TAKE DOMINION OVER YOUR EMOTIONS

30. *Check the mood you are in.* A check list helps you decide what your present mood is doing for you or against you. You see how strongly we are moved by moods that have nothing to do with logic or "common sense."

31. *How to give yourself the deep, lasting expectation of success.* A fascinating process of self-conditioning sends the confident expectation of success deep into your inmost being. You see, too, that the same process and an even faster process can give you full charge of any emotion.

32. *Give yourself postgraduate conditioning.* This process draws together two major elements of a well-lived life: success and health. Your conditioning now also extends to the "merry heart"—or basic cheerful optimism—that bulwarks you against much that might otherwise hurt.

IX. TACKLE YOUR PROBLEMS AND SOLVE THEM

33. *Define your problem carefully; state exactly what has to be done.* If you need a job, the way you state your problem has much to do with getting that job. Successful men state their problems in terms of expected success that point straight to a solution.

34. *Ask yourself: "Do I really want to solve this problem?"* Use key suggestions to search the emotional roots of

your problem; it may be doing something for you. Analyzing your problem can tell you a good deal about yourself and point the way to instant self-improvement.

35. *Formally evaluate the role of others in your problem.* In doing this you can arrive at the fairest possible solution to a problem that affects many people. Also you may realize that a "problem" person is having an effect upon your health.

X. FIND AND USE PLENTY OF ENERGY

36. *Check and see if you suffer the tiredness of indecision.* Most doubt is self-doubt, and as you take charge of your courage you rise above self-doubt and thus get rid of the energy-drain of indecision. You'll never be afraid of making an honest error; you know how to rise above it.

37. *Check and see if you suffer the tiredness of boredom.* All play and no work means boredom and fatigue; so does the job performed without interest or motivation. You get tired because you are tired of what is happening to you.

38. *Do you call anti-energy signals?* Every mind affects any other mind with which it communicates. An important check list shows how you may rob other people of energy at the same time as you rob yourself.

39. *When someone signals a negative, signal back a positive.* When you give people the impetus toward success, they take it eagerly. You also can communicate fatigue (or energy) without words, and a child will often take on the fatigue patterns of its father.

XI. YOU CAN BE SOVEREIGN OF YOURSELF

40. *Change the routines in your business life.* Finding a different way to handle your mail or arrange your desk can give you sharp new insight into the emotional bases of your actions, get you going on a new routine that brings out all you've got.

41. *Change your routine in other areas of your life.* Any change in routine, even reading a different newspaper, is a kind of broadening and refreshing "travel." Make

different friends. Listen to people whose opinions do not please you.

42. *Change the way you habitually react toward some person who makes you retreat.* Breaking some such routine can give you a great breakthrough in all your human relations, and thus a great breakthrough in success.

43. *A check list gives you insight into possible childhood influences.* A person wedded to his Will to Lose may use such influences as an excuse for failure; but you know the door to success is never locked, and we are never failures save if we make ourselves so.

A Note About the Author

"J. K. SUMMERHILL" *is the pen name of a writer and businessman who has worked in many fields and many places. He and his wife have now settled in Manhattan, in a beautifully restored old brownstone house that is the center of much business, literary and social activity.*

Mr. Summerhill's career began when—as a poor man's son—he went to work at fourteen in a department store's mail room. It was in this first job that he developed and used his now famous "work level, pay level" technique which since has guided many other men to swift, sure advancement. At that time it led him to invent a more efficient way of delivering packages to the post office; it earned him his first raise and soon he took full charge of himself and his own earnings potential.

Mr. Summerhill put himself through college with the proceeds from a variety of jobs that included being a lifeguard, a door-to-door salesman of pots and pans, and a writer of magazine articles (which he wrote while babysitting). Upon graduation he became a speech writer for a well-known political figure; then an advertising copywriter. He mapped out several successful campaigns which have become models of effective advertising.

Later, Mr. Summerhill moved on to meet new challenges in real estate, retail selling and other areas. More importantly, from his own point of view, his studies in psychology and business methods led him into the role of personnel trouble-shooter for several companies. It was in this work that he finally formalized and proved his techniques for personal success that work for any man, anywhere.

"If I am proud of anything," he says, "I am proud of having

197

shown so many men how to make money while they succeeded at the same time in fulfilling themselves as individuals. The man who has a lot of money in his pockets and nothing in his soul is just another moneybags. The man who is a real individual, who enjoys being himself, and who also has money enough to lift him above money worry, is the man who really makes something out of his life."

The great theme of TAKE CHARGE OF YOUR LIFE had to brew many years in J. K. Summerhill's subconscious before he was ready to put it into print. It is based on both his own experiences and the experiences of others—where, in most cases, he had a hand in forming those experiences. Mr. Summerhill finds he writes more fluently when he puts himself into stories, and suggests that the reader accept "I" even where another writer might use "he"—as long as the carefully selected stories make their points. In fact, he says, the reader is welcome to consider that "I" includes himself, to help him all the more deeply to live the experience told in each story.

Now semiretired, Mr. Summerhill limits his working time to twenty hours a week. He spends his winters sailing in southern waters, preferably with a couple of grandchildren on deck.

Concerning his age, Mr. Summerhill will say only that he was born when the twentieth century was young. When he reaches eighty-five, he says, he will put his feet on his desk and catch up on his reading.